DIVER DETAILS

Name

I0197603

Address

Telephone

Email

Club/School	Membership No.

Diving Qualifications

Log Book No.

If you find this log book please contact the owner using the details above

ISBN 978-1-909455-19-1 Diving Log Book (Northern Waters)
ISBN 978-1-909455-20-7 Diving Log Book (Sharks)
ISBN 978-1-909455-21-4 Diving Log Book (Under the Sea)

© **2018, 2020 Dived Up Publications**. All intellectual property and associated rights are hereby asserted and reserved by Dived Up Publications in full compliance with UK, European and international law. No part of this log book may be copied, reproduced, stored in any retrieval system or transmitted in any form or by any means, including in hard copy or via the internet, without the prior written permission of the publishers to whom all such rights have been assigned worldwide.

Cover design © Dived Up Publications. Original artwork by Bethan Buss.

Published 2020 by
Dived Up Publications
Oxford, United Kingdom
Email info@divedup.com
Web www.DivedUp.com

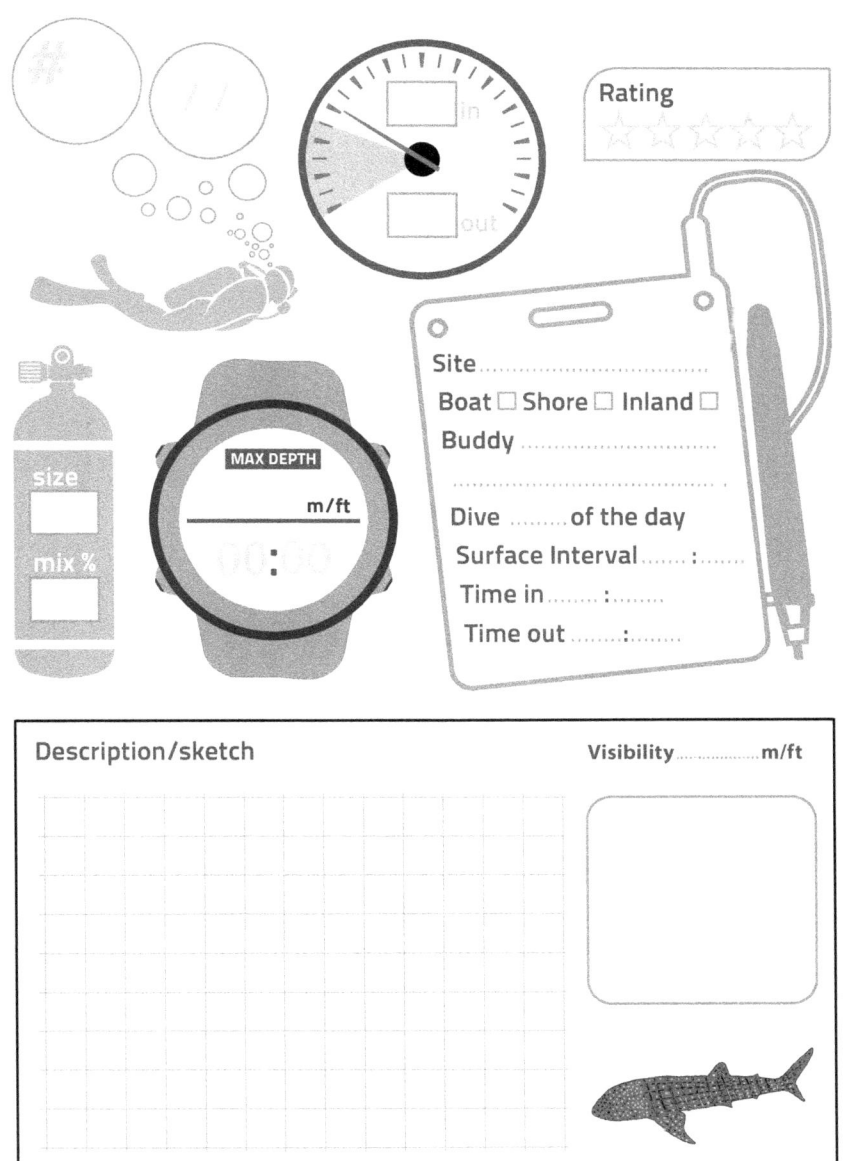

Rating

Site..................................
Boat ☐ Shore ☐ Inland ☐
Buddy ....
....
Dive .... of the day
Surface Interval .... : ....
Time in .... : ....
Time out .... : ....

size

mix %

MAX DEPTH
m/ft

in
out

Description/sketch

Visibility .... m/ft

Accumulated Dive Time

Milestone

Verified by

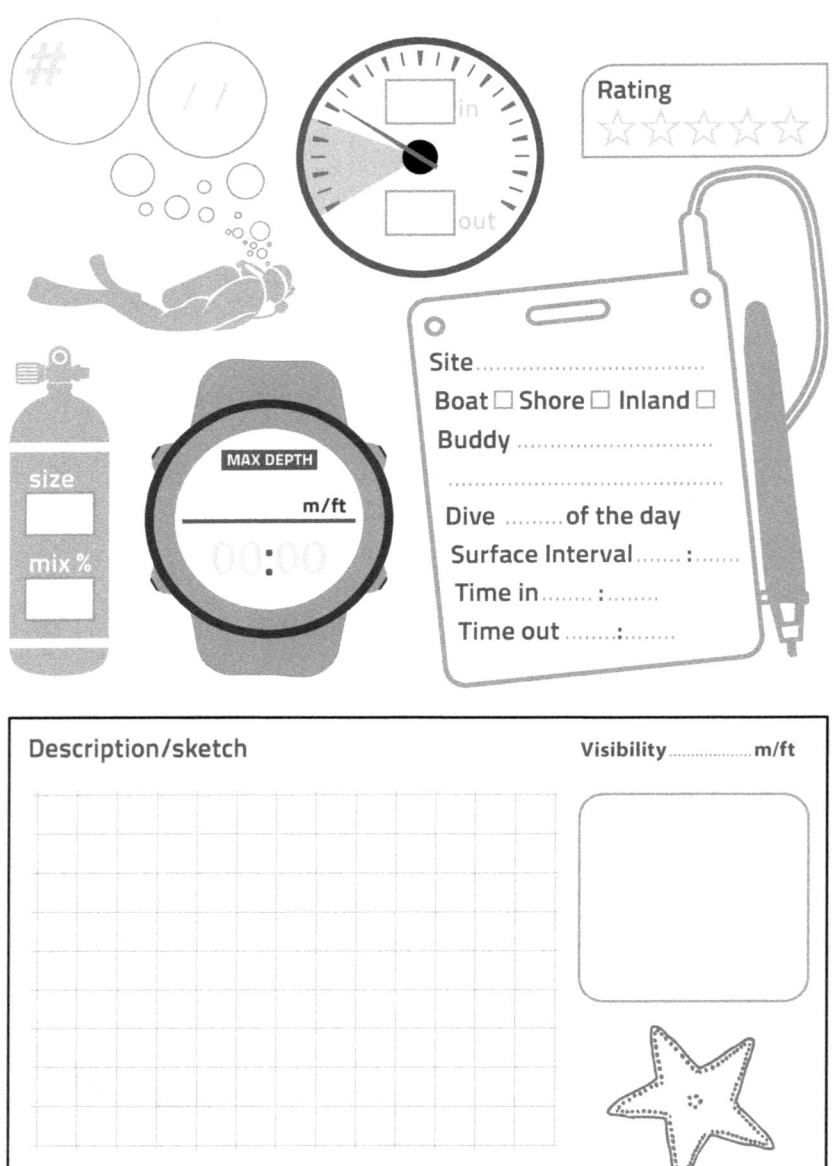

Site..........................
Boat ☐ Shore ☐ Inland ☐
Buddy ....
....
Dive .... of the day
Surface Interval .... : ....
Time in .... : ....
Time out .... : ....

MAX DEPTH
m/ft
00:00

Rating
☆☆☆☆☆

size

mix %

Description/sketch   Visibility .... m/ft

Accumulated Dive Time   Milestone   Verified by
.... : ....

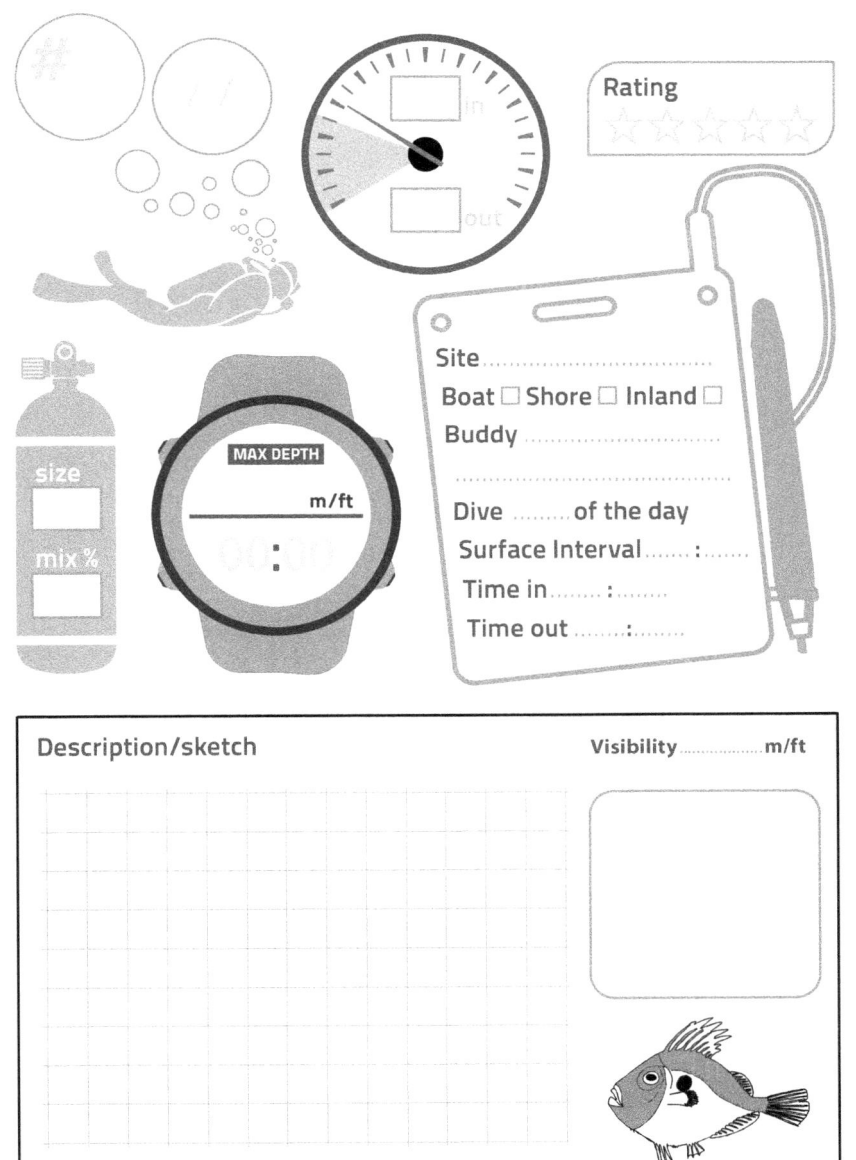

Rating

Site..................................
Boat ☐ Shore ☐ Inland ☐
Buddy ....

Dive .... of the day
Surface Interval .... : ....
Time in .... : ....
Time out .... : ....

size

mix %

MAX DEPTH

m/ft

Description/sketch

Visibility .... m/ft

Accumulated Dive Time   Milestone   Verified by

.... : ....

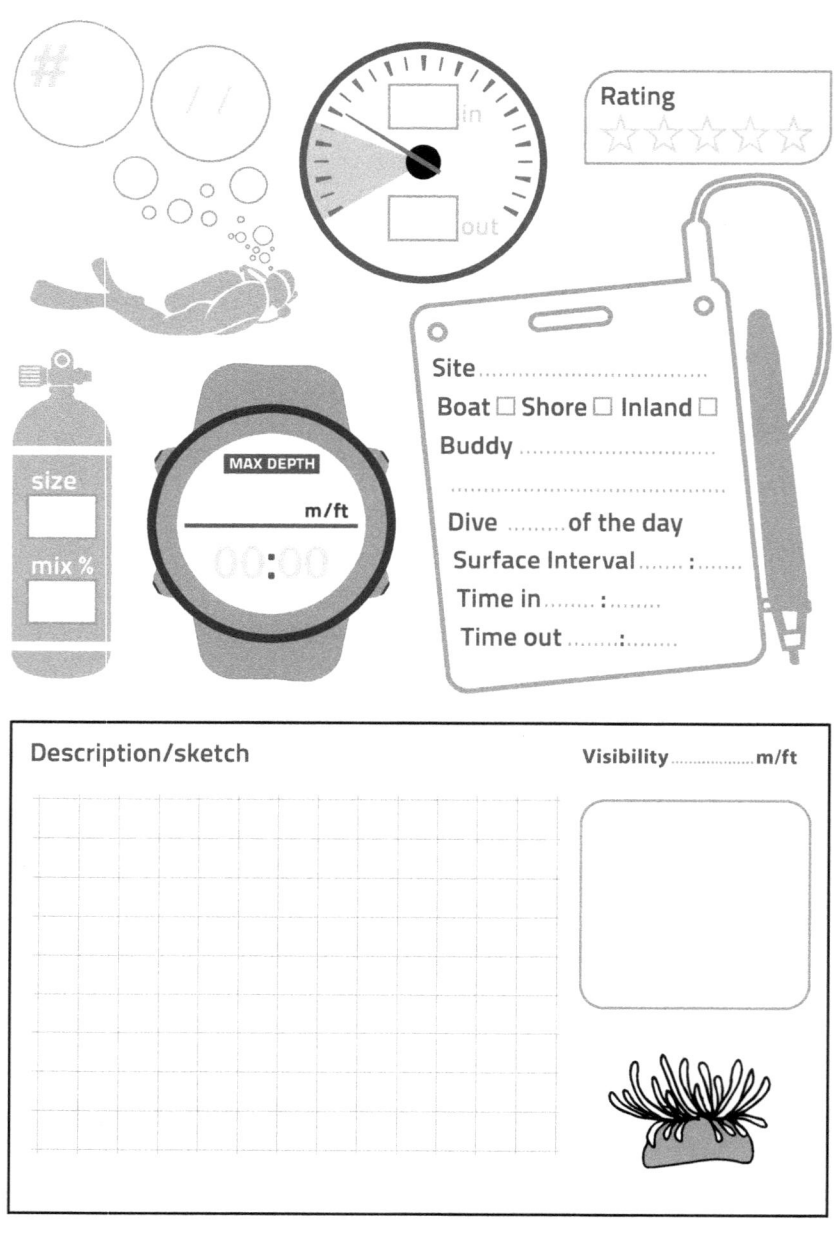

Rating
☆☆☆☆☆

in
out

size

mix %

MAX DEPTH
m/ft
00:00

Site..........................
Boat ☐ Shore ☐ Inland ☐
Buddy........................
....
Dive .... of the day
Surface Interval .... : ....
Time in .... : ....
Time out .... : ....

Description/sketch

Visibility .... m/ft

Accumulated Dive Time

.... : ....

Milestone

Verified by

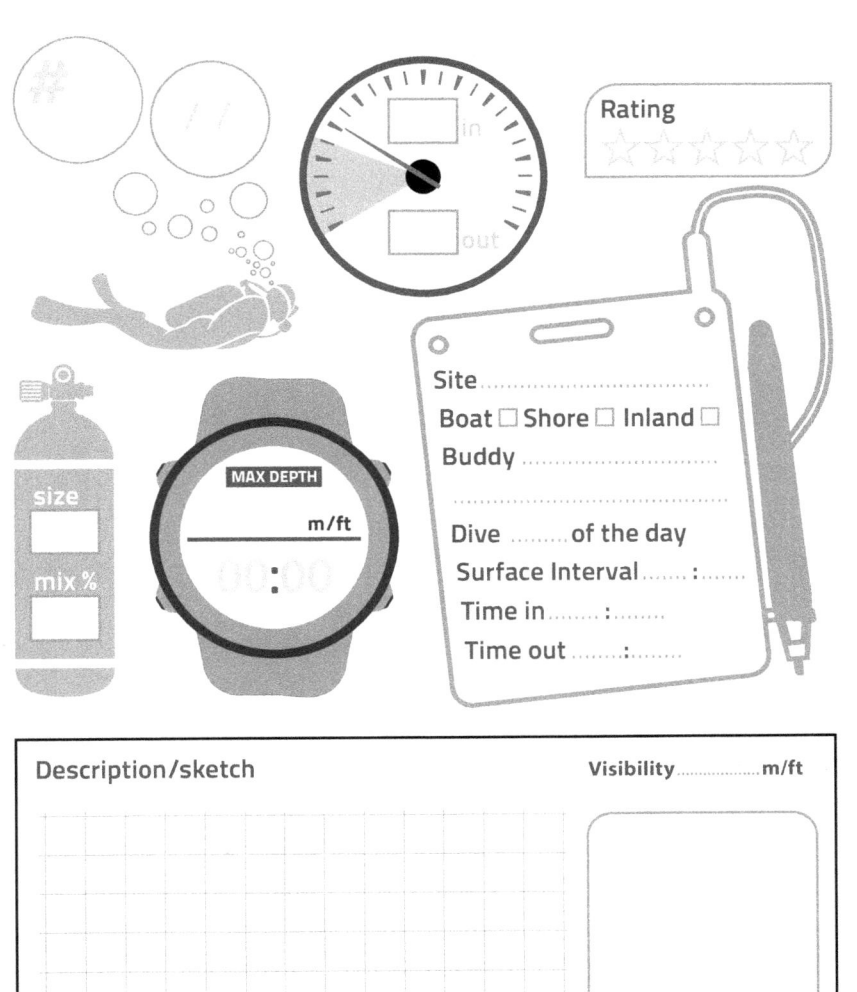

in
out

Rating
☆☆☆☆☆

size

mix %

MAX DEPTH
_____ m/ft
00:00

Site....................................
Boat ☐ Shore ☐ Inland ☐
Buddy ....
....
Dive .... of the day
Surface Interval .... : ....
Time in .... : ....
Time out .... : ....

Description/sketch

Visibility .... m/ft

Accumulated Dive Time

.... : ....

Milestone

Verified by

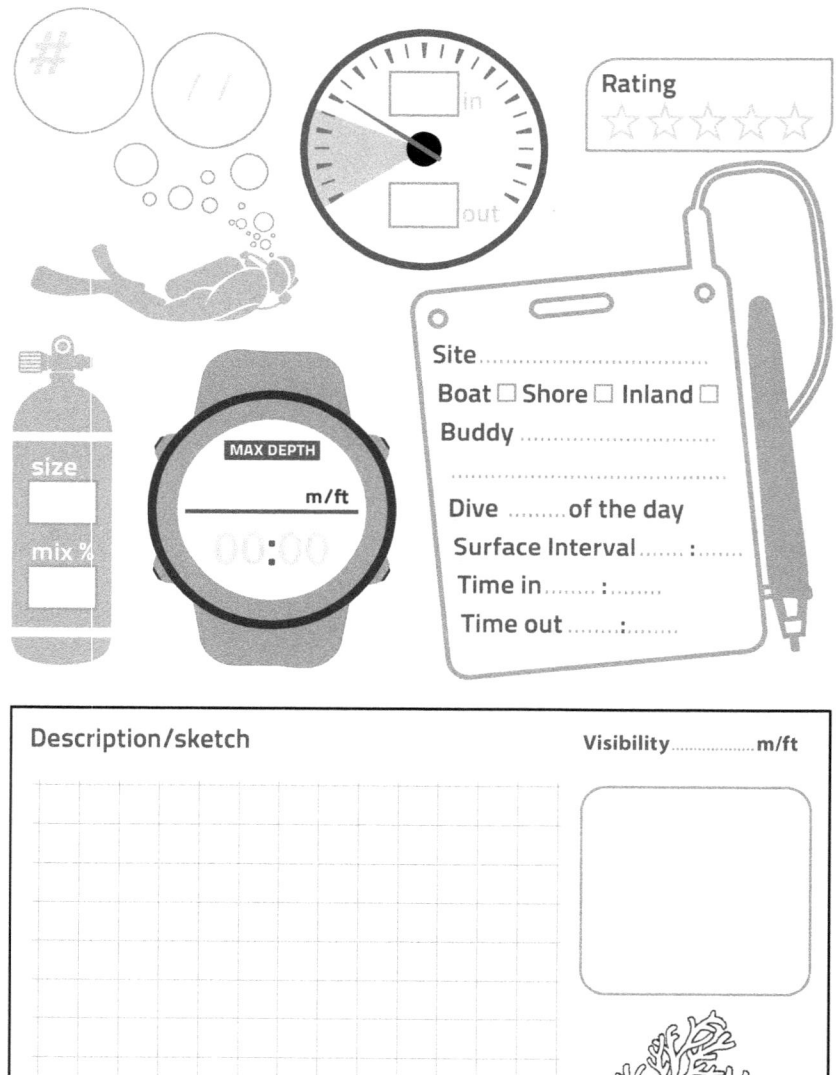

Site..........................
Boat ☐ Shore ☐ Inland ☐
Buddy ....

Dive .... of the day
Surface Interval .... : ....
Time in .... : ....
Time out .... : ....

MAX DEPTH
m/ft

Rating

Description/sketch

Visibility .... m/ft

Accumulated Dive Time

Milestone

Verified by

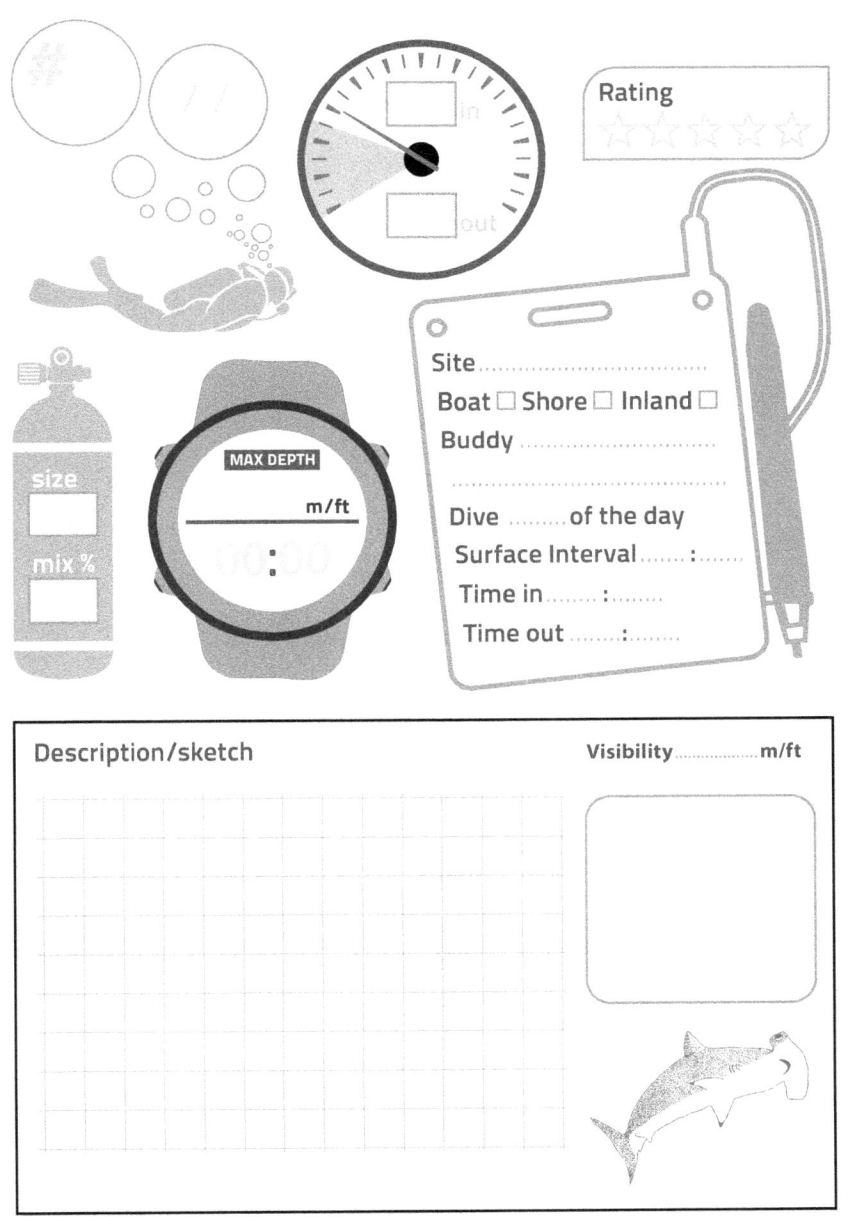

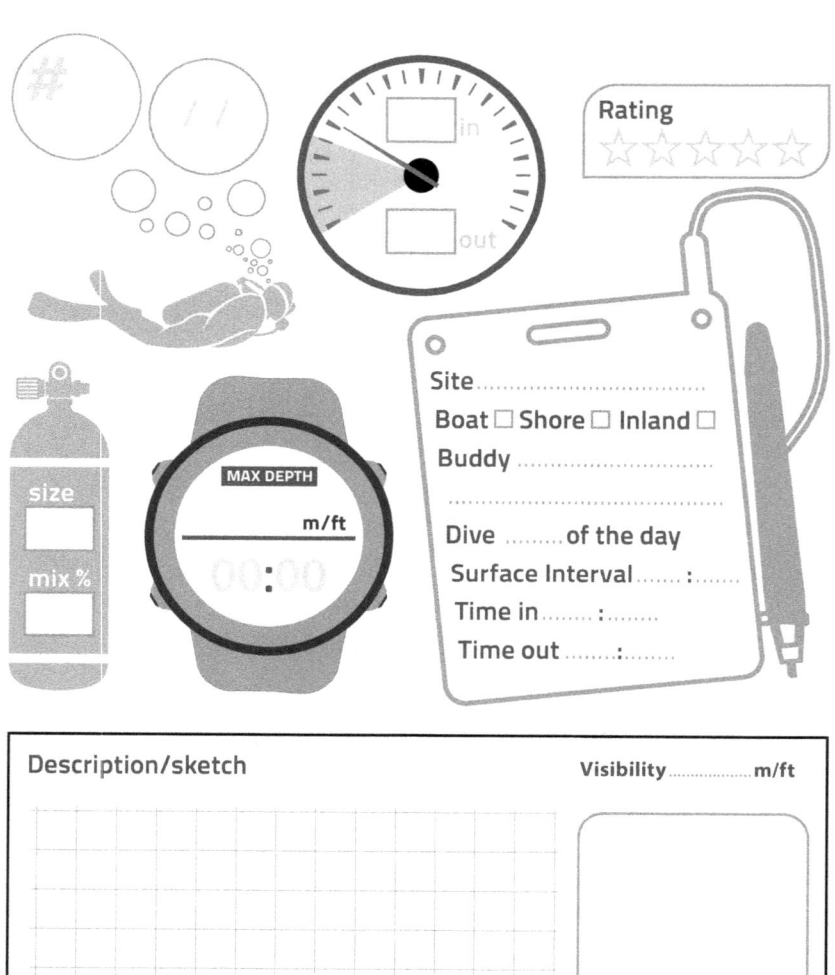

Site ....
Boat ☐ Shore ☐ Inland ☐
Buddy ....
....
Dive .... of the day
Surface Interval .... : ....
Time in .... : ....
Time out .... : ....

MAX DEPTH
m/ft

size
mix %

Rating
☆☆☆☆☆

Description/sketch

Visibility .... m/ft

Accumulated Dive Time

.... : ....

Milestone

....

Verified by

....

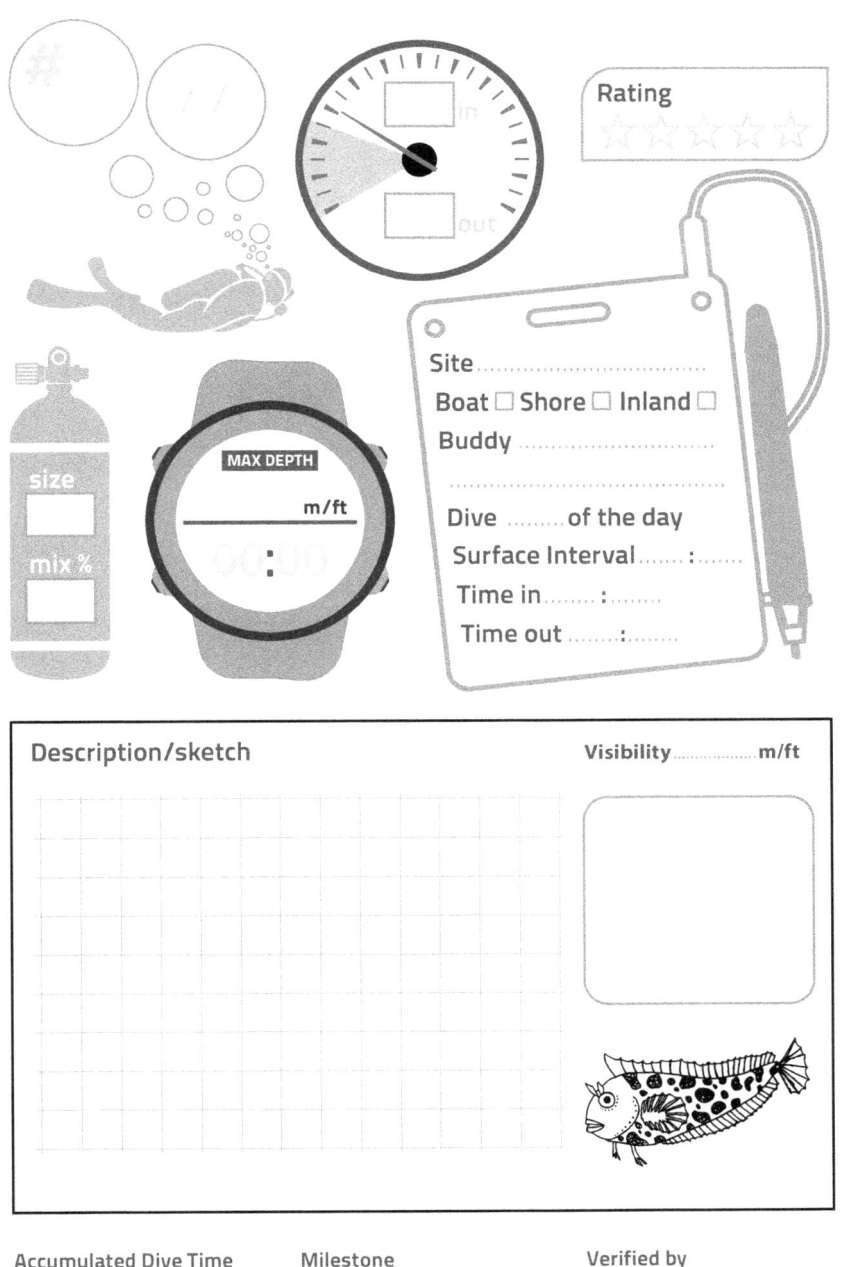

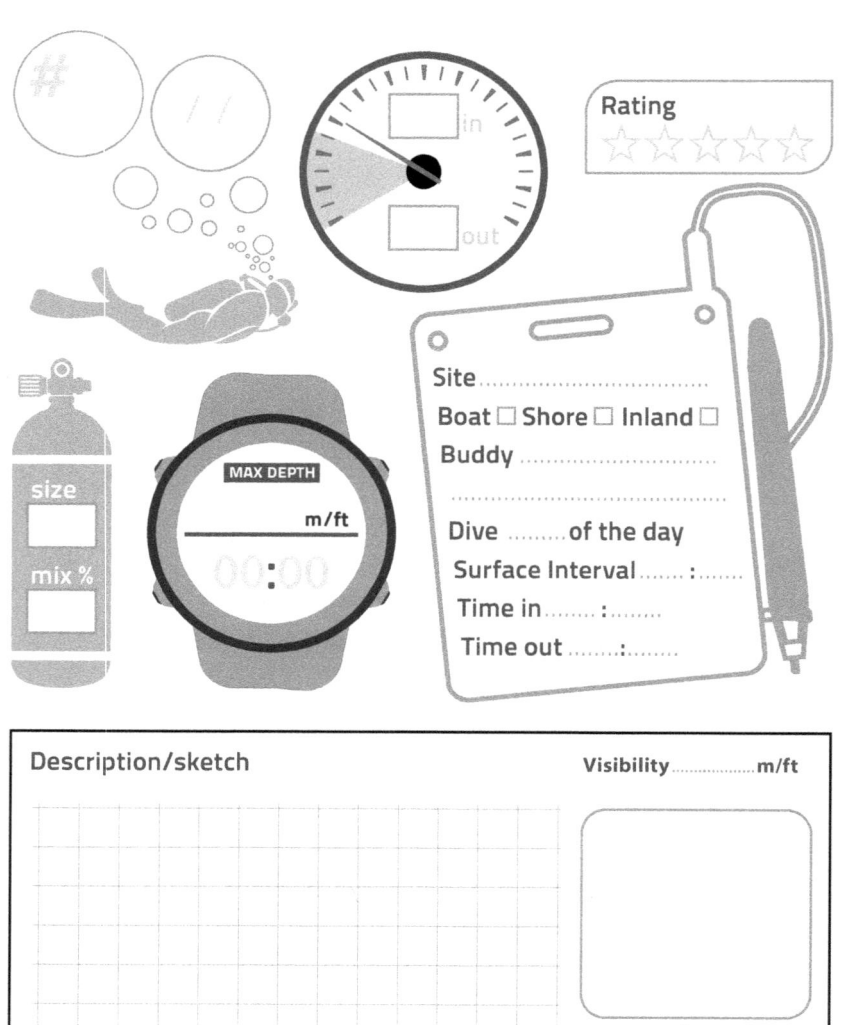

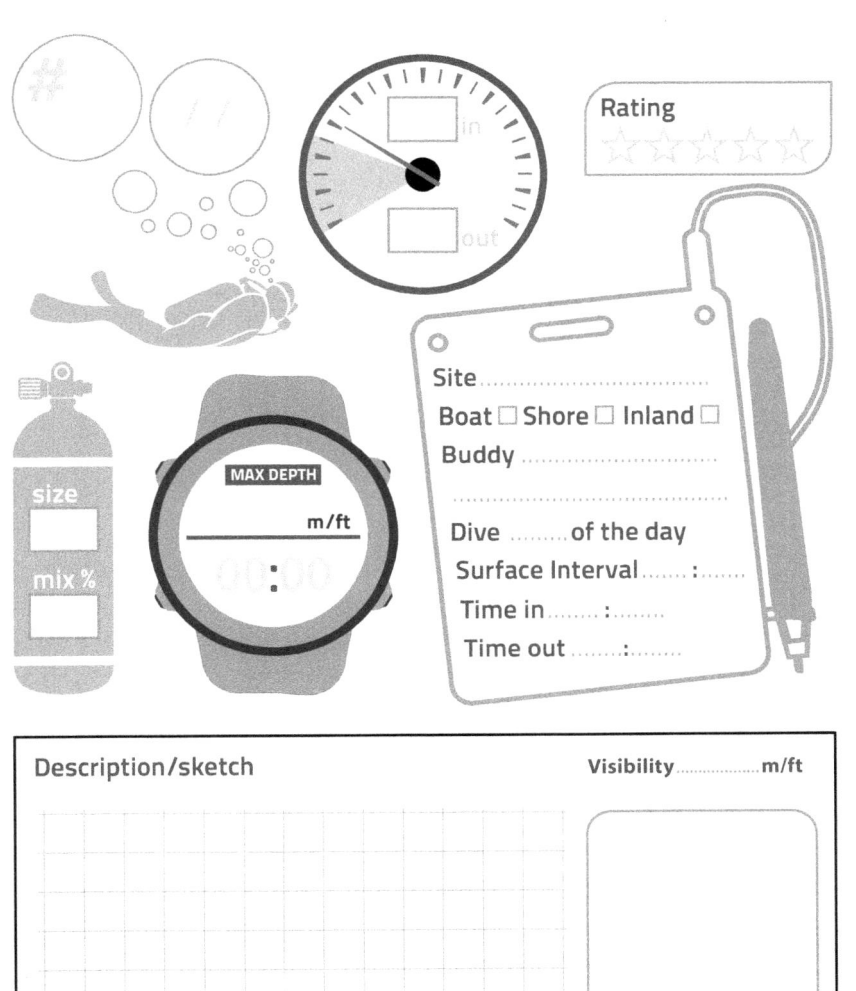

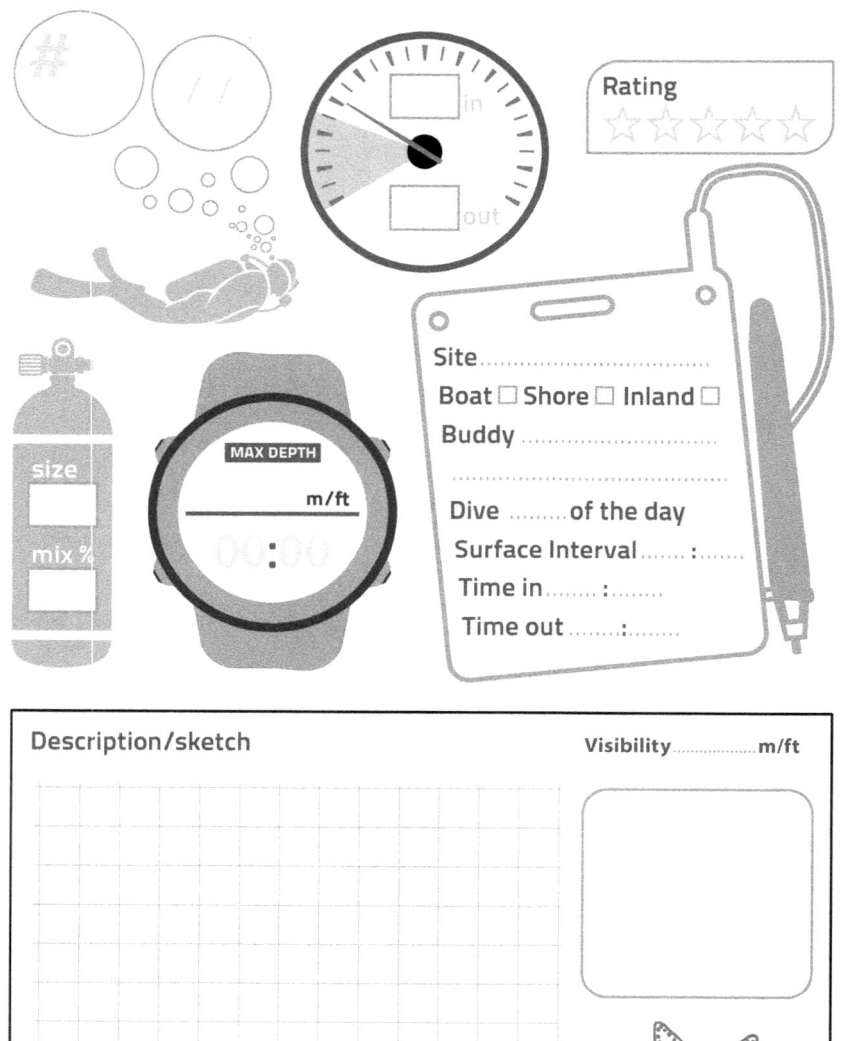

size

mix %

Rating ☆☆☆☆☆

Site..................................
Boat ☐ Shore ☐ Inland ☐
Buddy ....
....
Dive .... of the day
Surface Interval .... : ......
Time in .... : ......
Time out .... : ......

MAX DEPTH
m/ft

Description/sketch

Visibility .... m/ft

Accumulated Dive Time

Milestone

Verified by

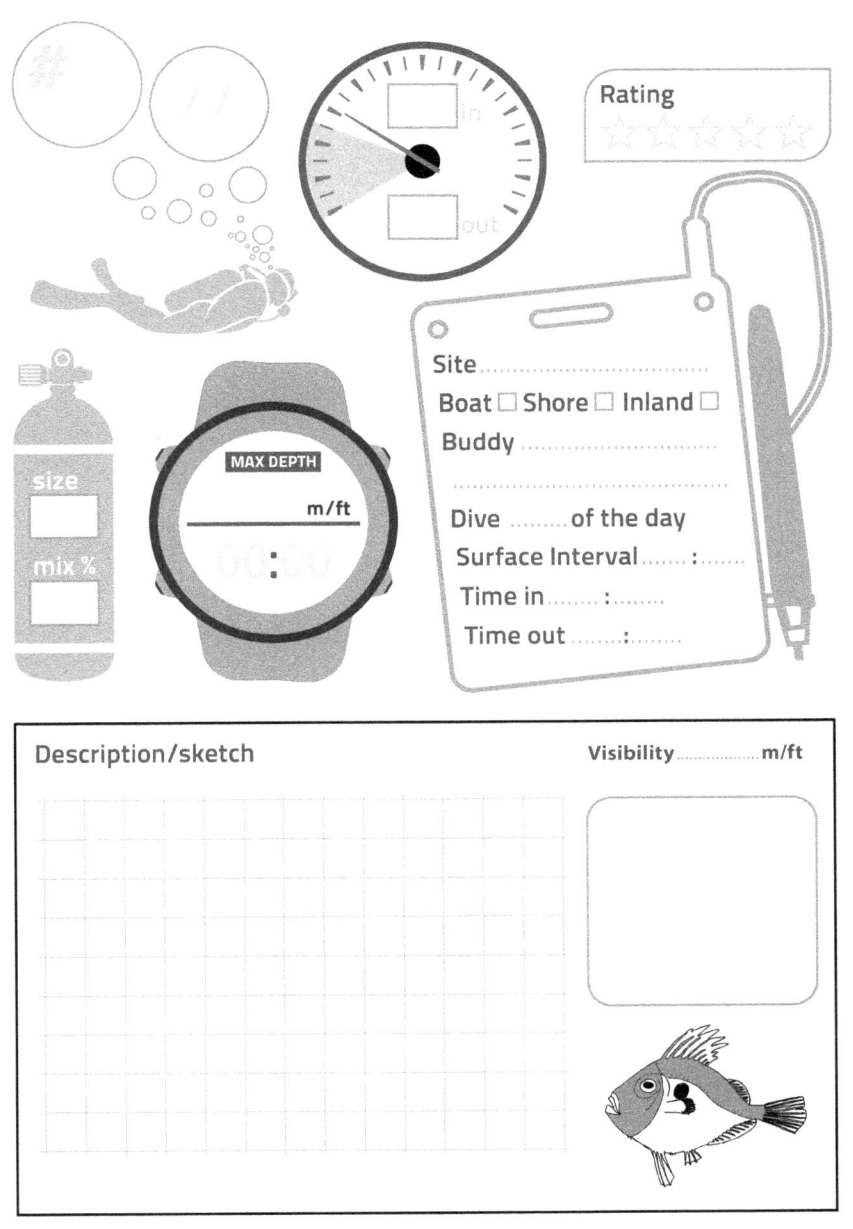

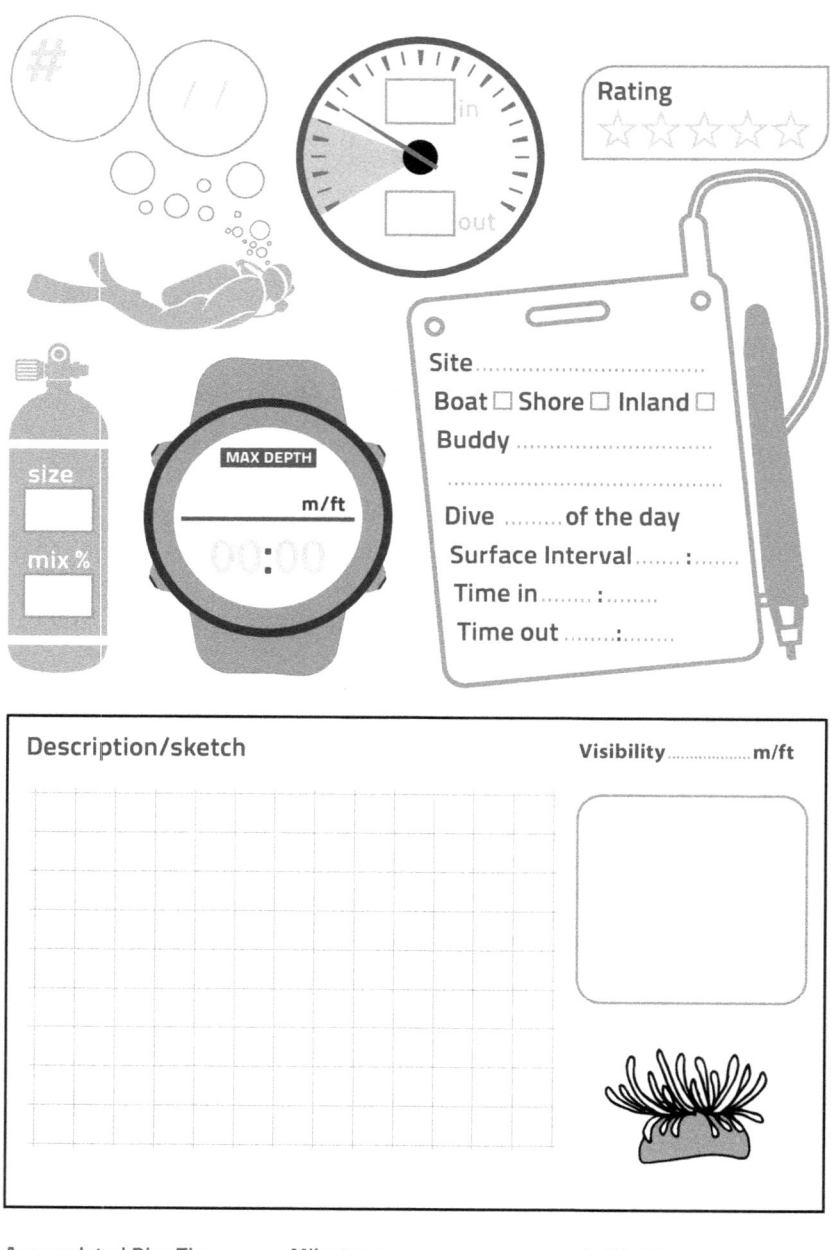

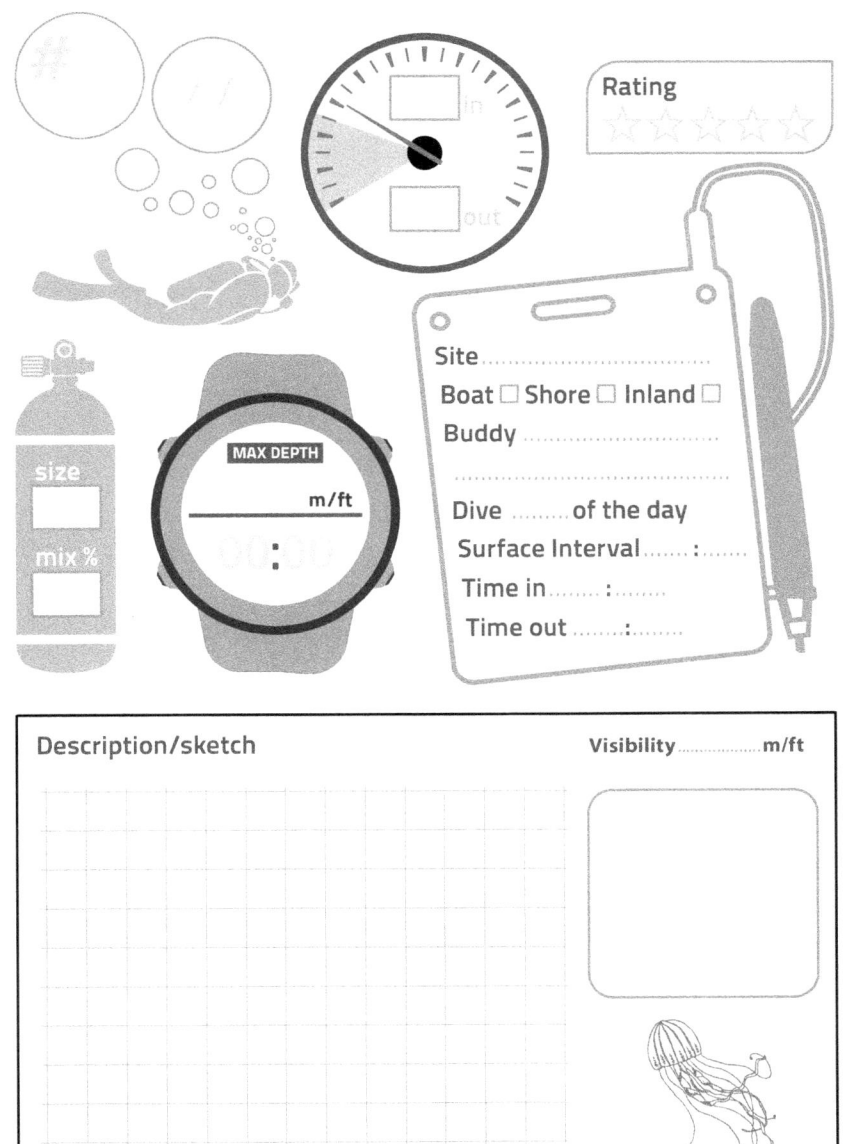

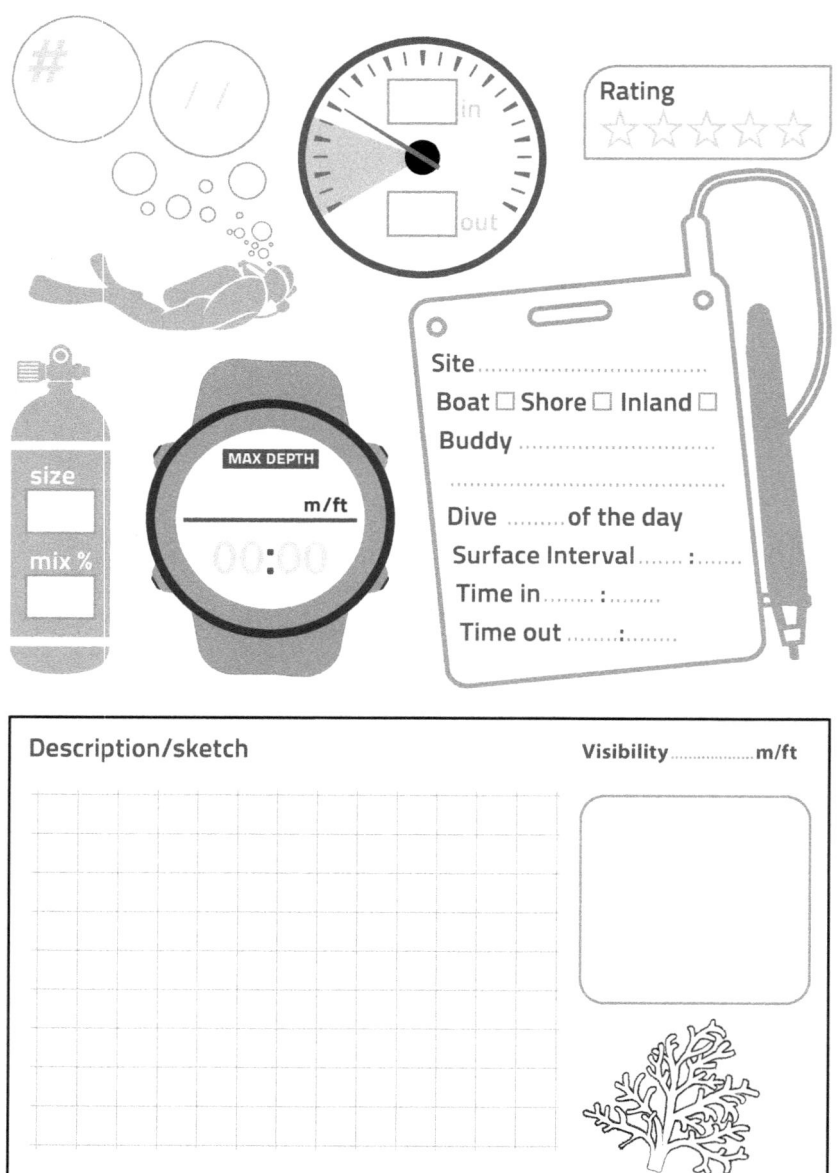

Rating ☆☆☆☆☆

in
out

size
mix %

MAX DEPTH
m/ft
00:00

Site ....
Boat ☐ Shore ☐ Inland ☐
Buddy ....
....
Dive .... of the day
Surface Interval .... : ....
Time in .... : ....
Time out .... : ....

Description/sketch

Visibility .... m/ft

Accumulated Dive Time
.... : ....

Milestone
....

Verified by
....

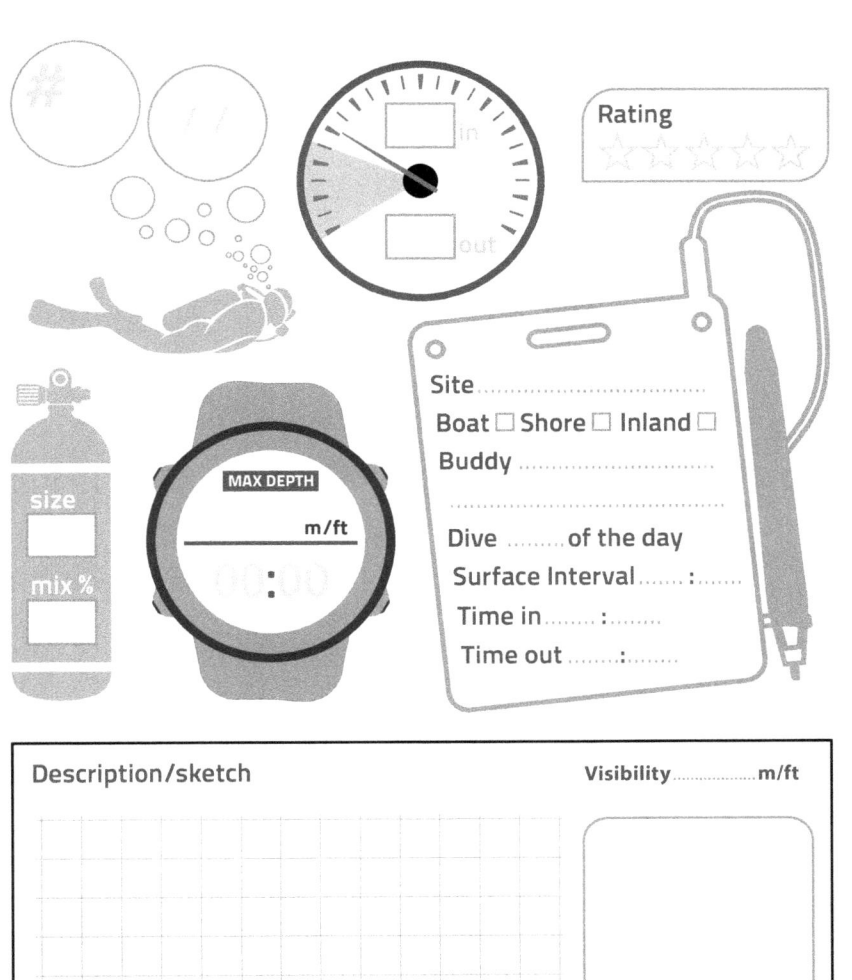

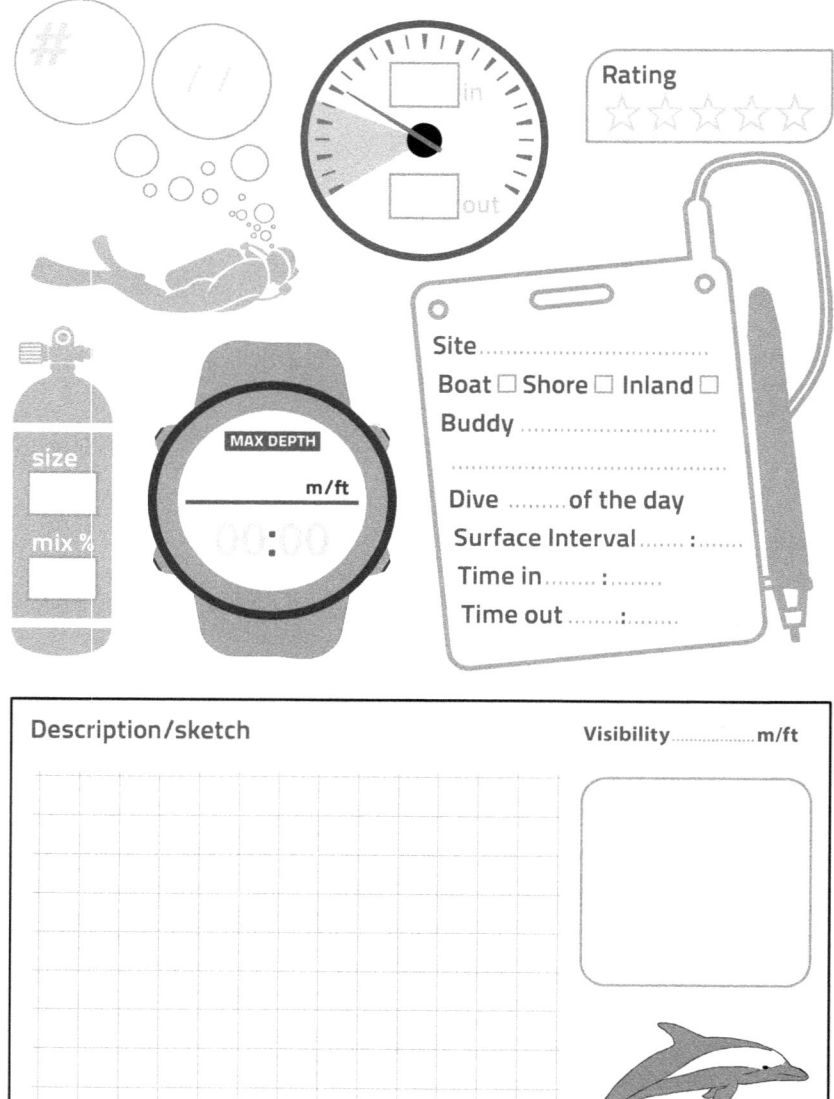

Site..........................
Boat ☐ Shore ☐ Inland ☐
Buddy ....

Dive .... of the day
Surface Interval .... : ....
Time in .... : ....
Time out .... : ....

size
mix %

MAX DEPTH
m/ft

Rating ☆☆☆☆☆

Description/sketch   Visibility .... m/ft

Accumulated Dive Time   Milestone   Verified by

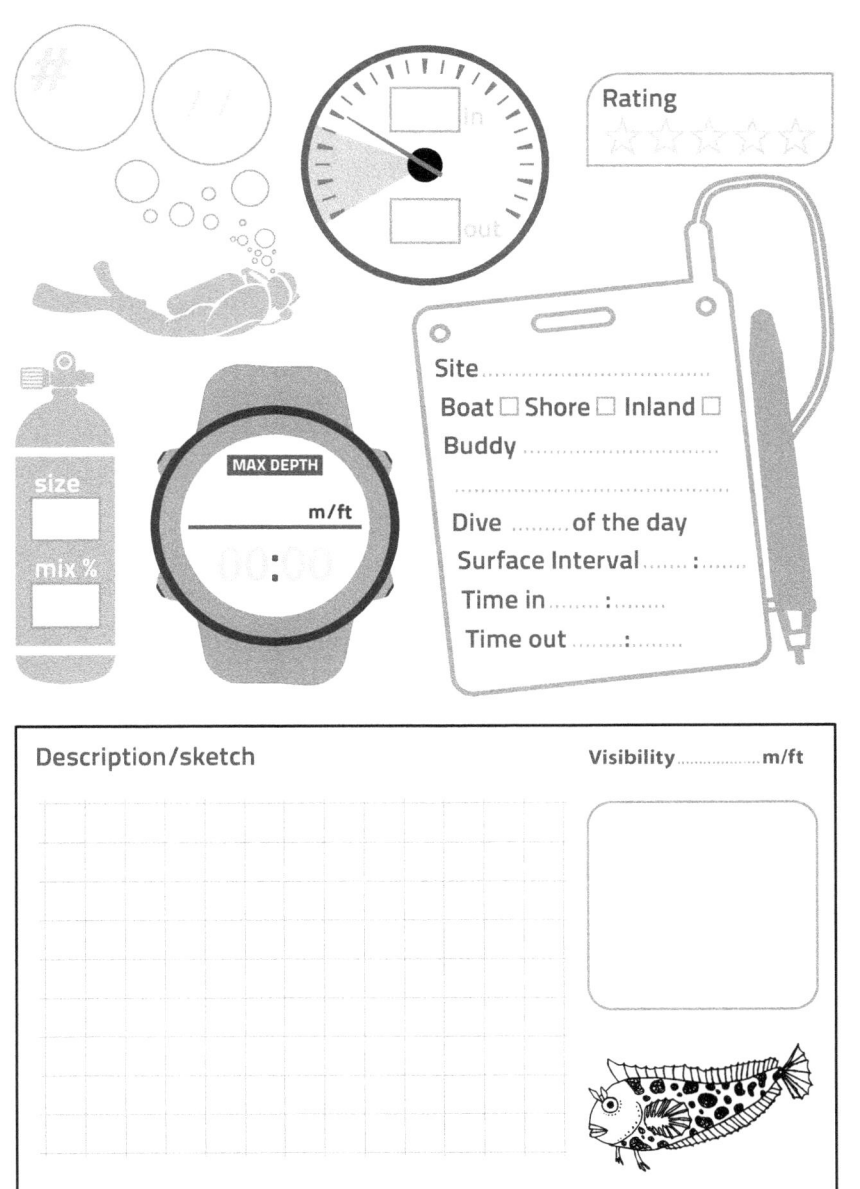

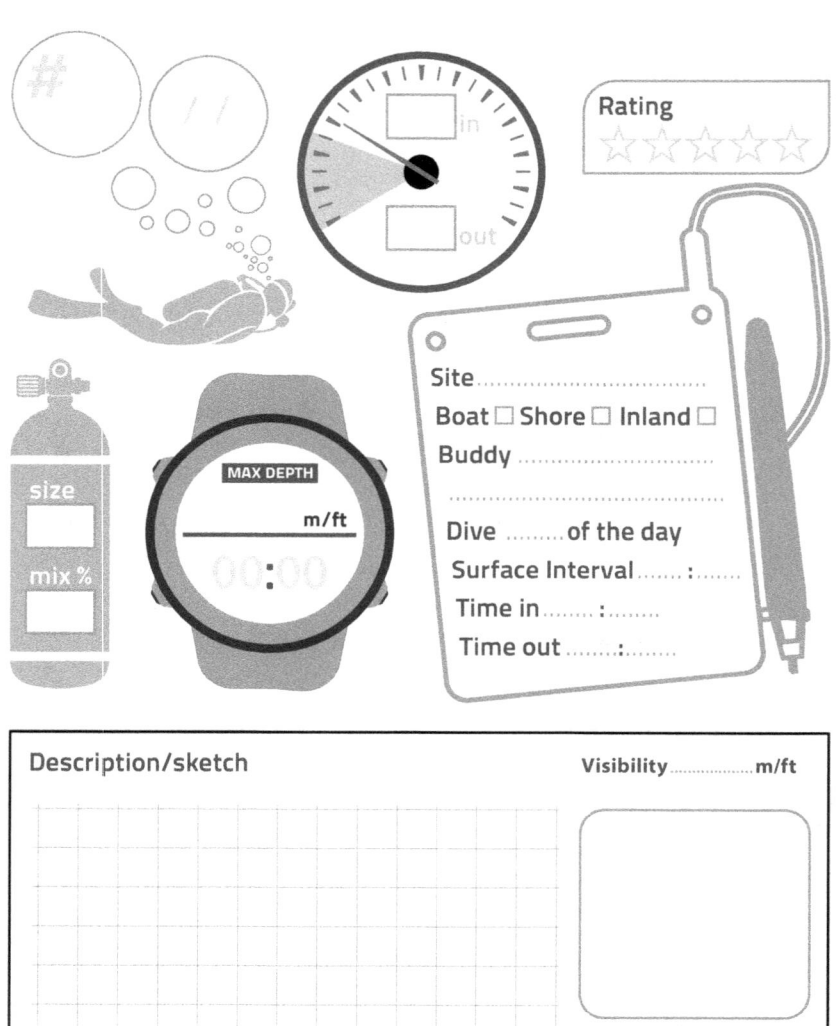

Site ....
Boat ☐ Shore ☐ Inland ☐
Buddy ....
....
Dive .... of the day
Surface Interval .... : ....
Time in .... : ....
Time out .... : ....

Rating

MAX DEPTH
m/ft
00:00

size
mix %

Description/sketch

Visibility .... m/ft

Accumulated Dive Time
.... : ....

Milestone

Verified by

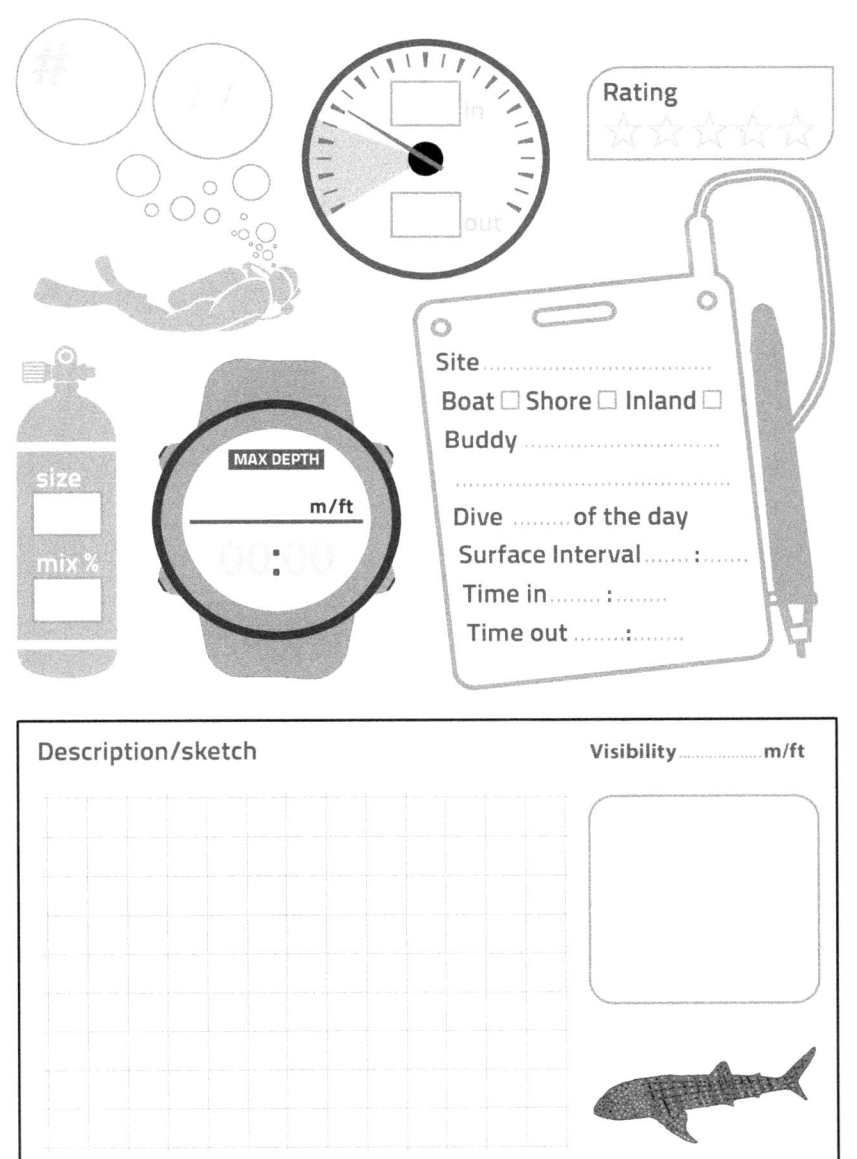

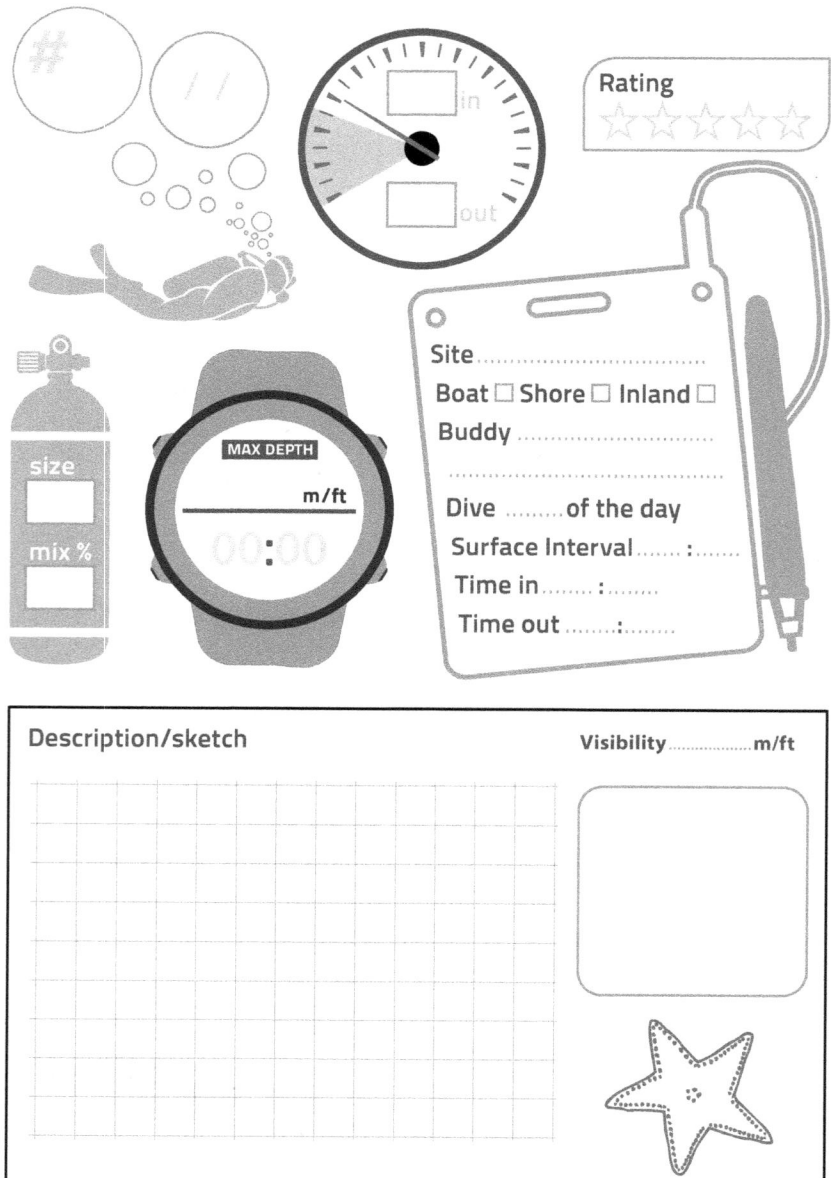

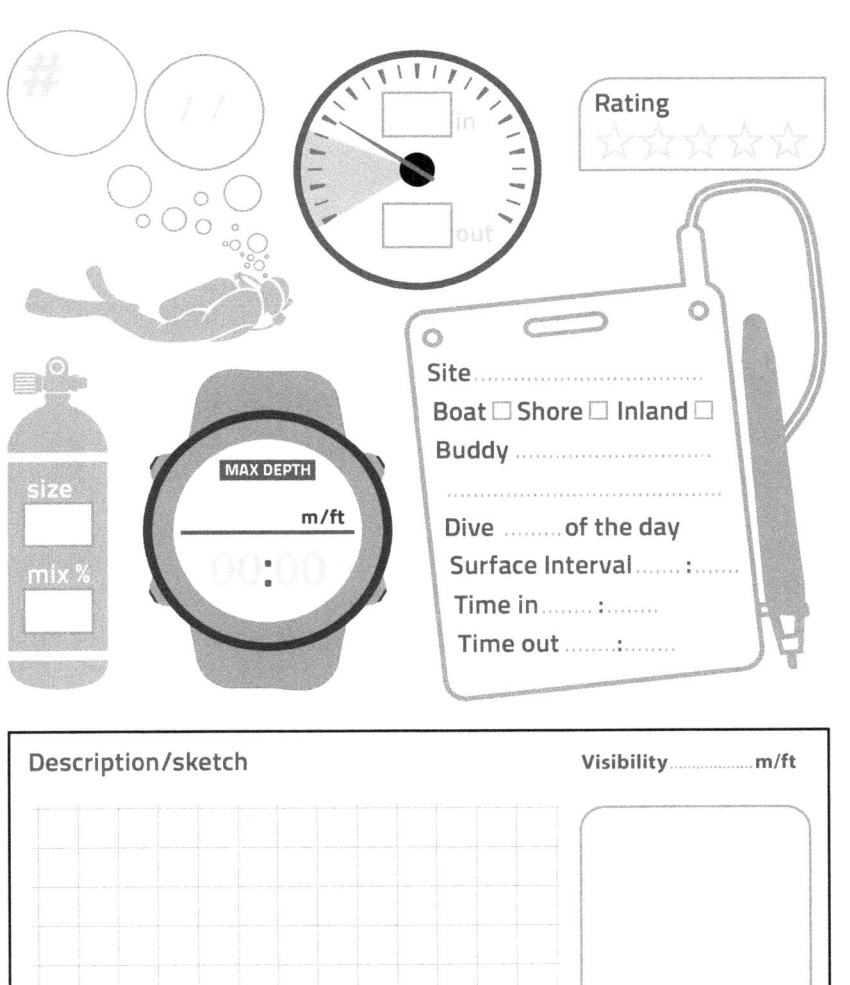

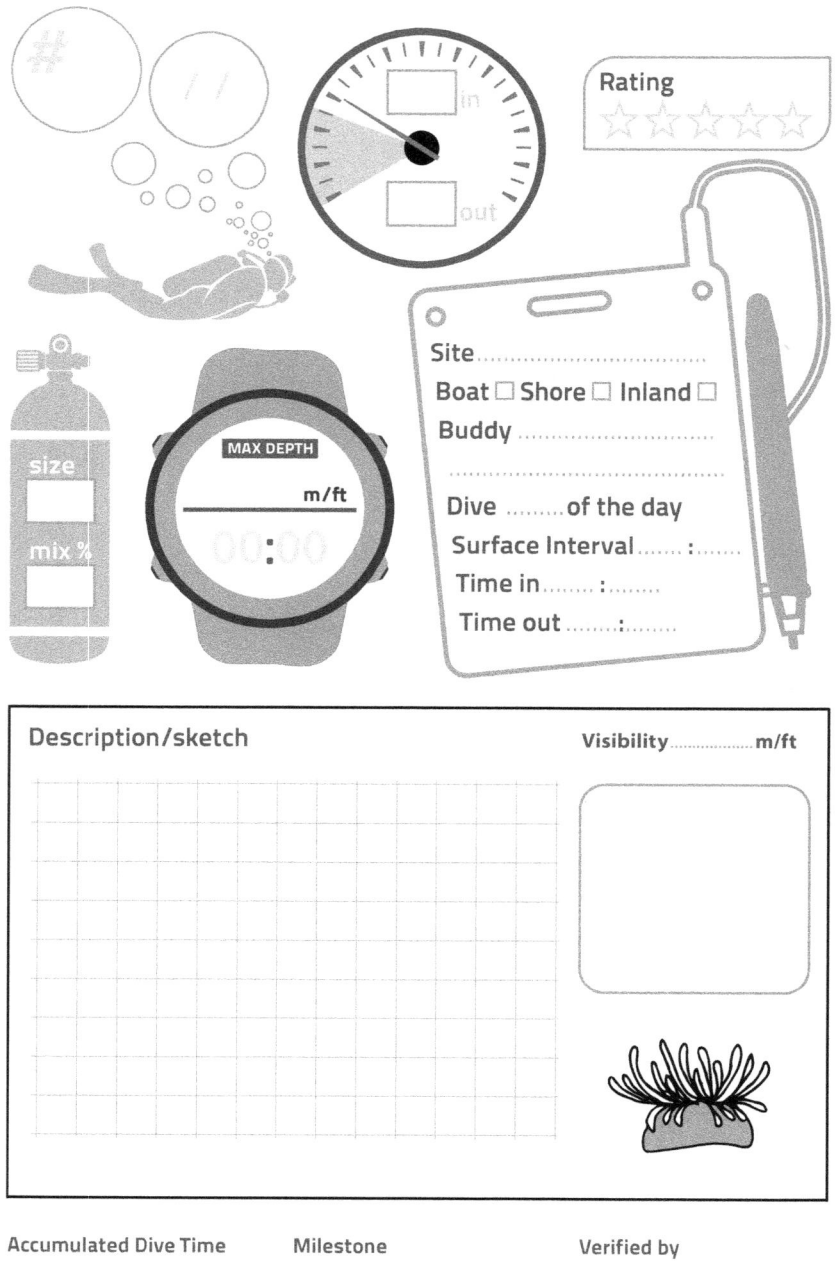

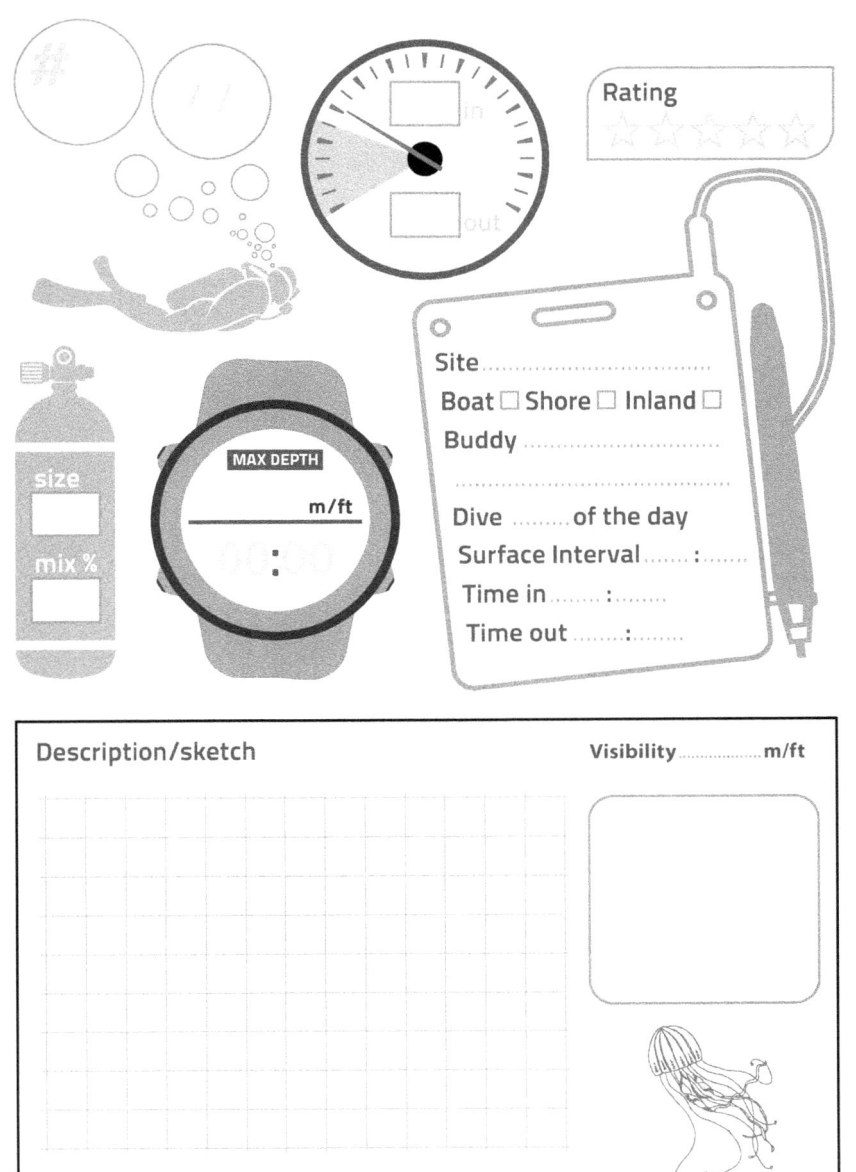

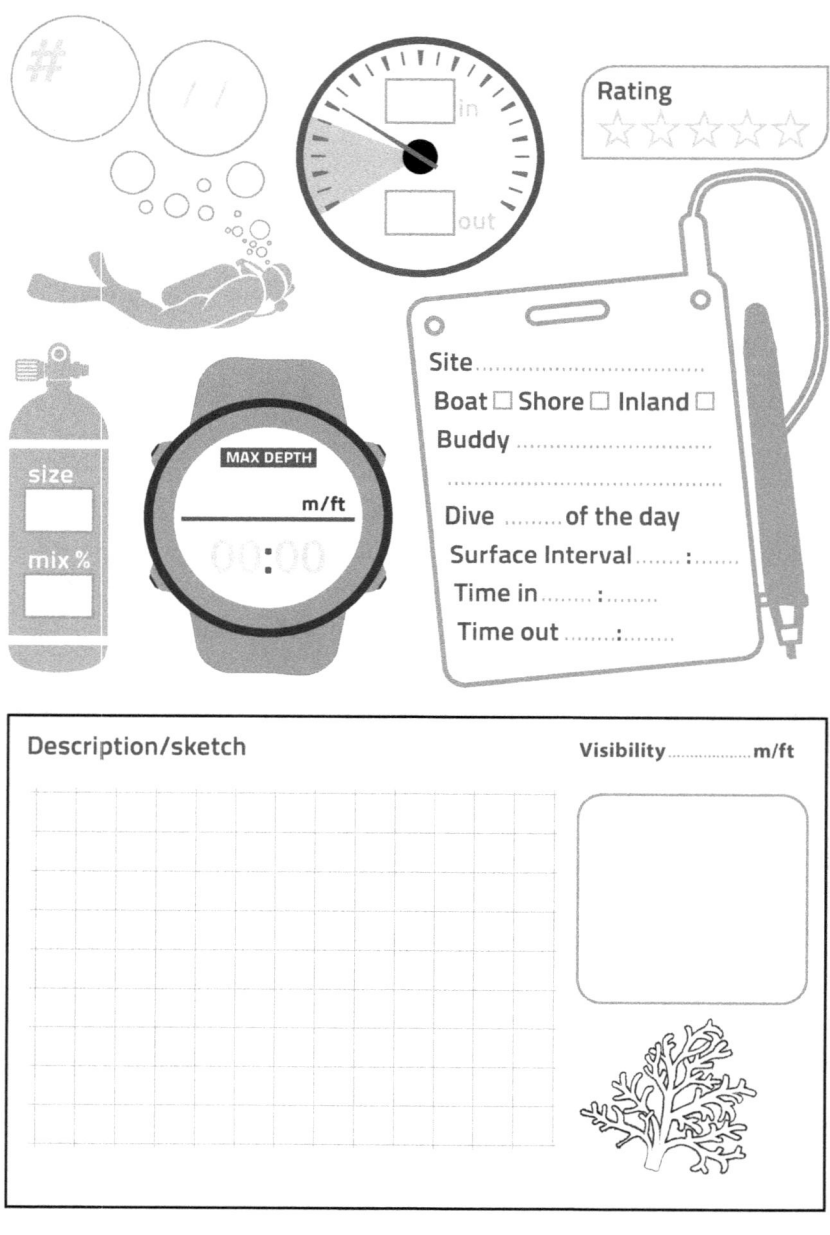

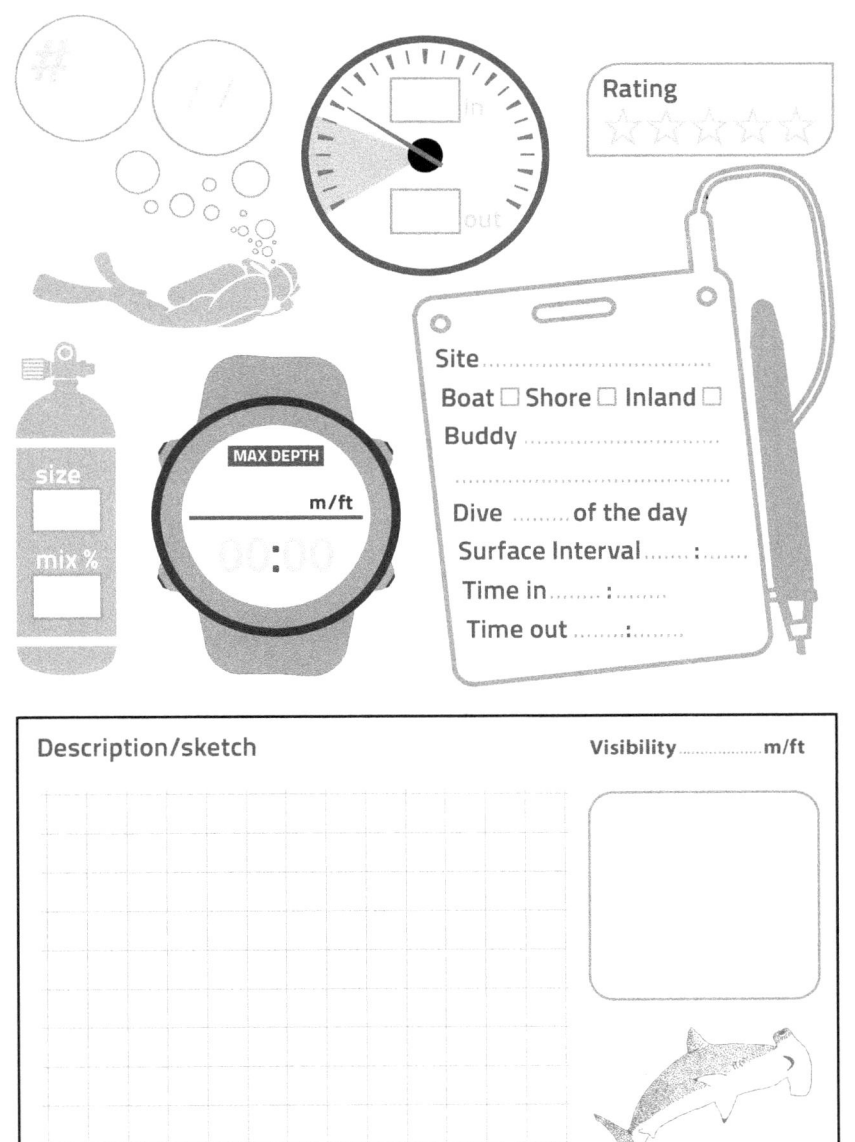

Site..........................
Boat ☐ Shore ☐ Inland ☐
Buddy ....

Dive .... of the day
Surface Interval .... : ....
Time in .... : ....
Time out .... : ....

Rating ☆☆☆☆☆

MAX DEPTH .... m/ft

size
mix %

Description/sketch

Visibility .... m/ft

Accumulated Dive Time
.... : ....

Milestone

Verified by

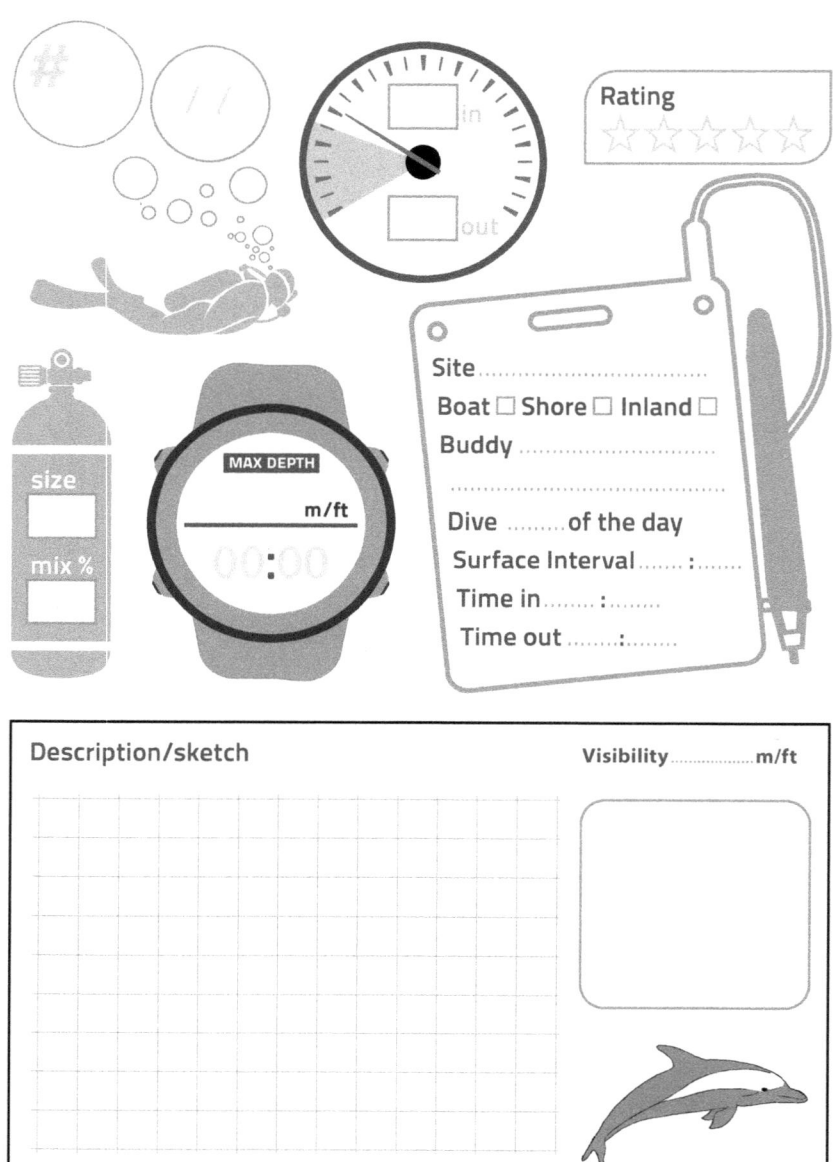

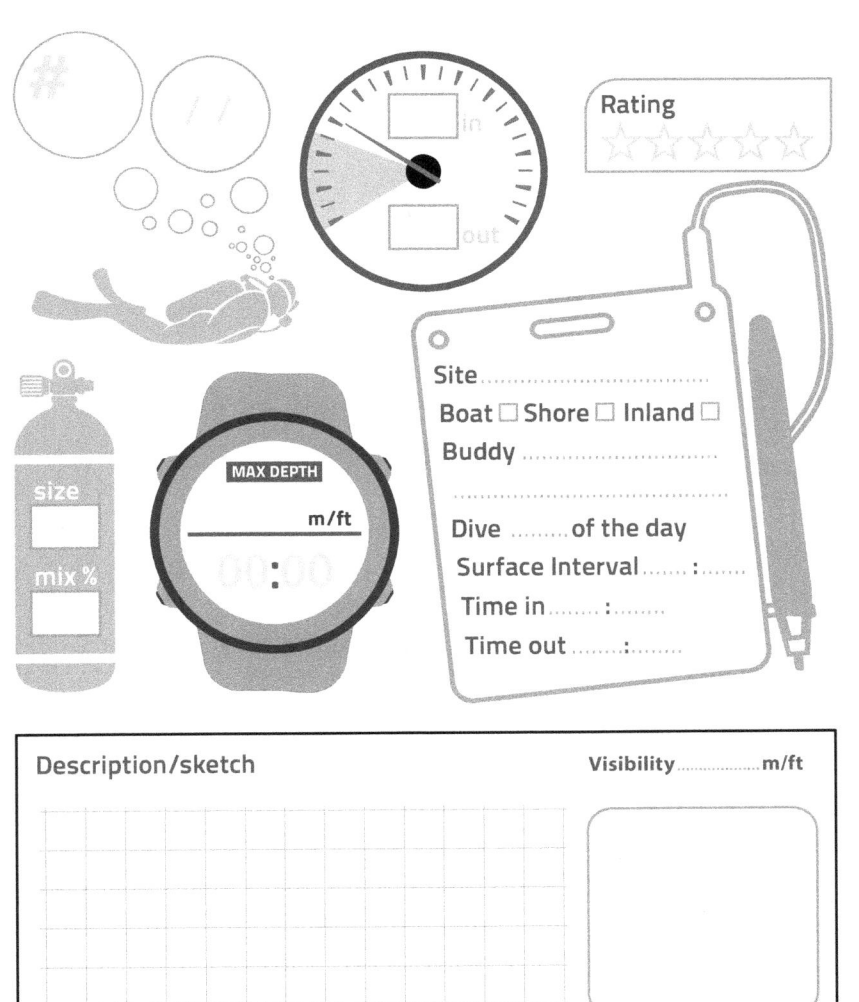

Rating ☆☆☆☆☆

size

mix %

MAX DEPTH
m/ft
00:00

Site..........................
Boat ☐ Shore ☐ Inland ☐
Buddy ....
....
Dive .... of the day
Surface Interval .... : ....
Time in .... : ....
Time out .... : ....

Description/sketch   Visibility .... m/ft

Accumulated Dive Time   Milestone   Verified by

.... : ....

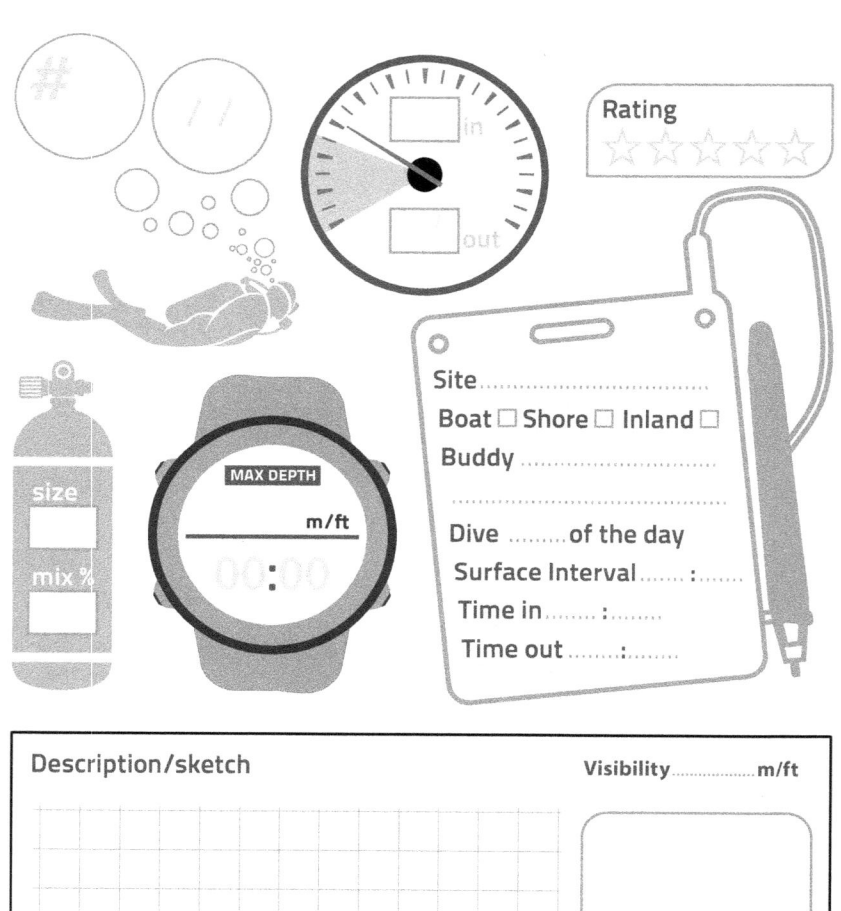

Site......................................
Boat ☐ Shore ☐ Inland ☐
Buddy ....
....
Dive .... of the day
Surface Interval .... : ....
Time in .... : ....
Time out .... : ....

MAX DEPTH
m/ft
00:00

size
mix %

Rating
☆☆☆☆☆

Description/sketch   Visibility .... m/ft

Accumulated Dive Time   Milestone   Verified by
.... : ....

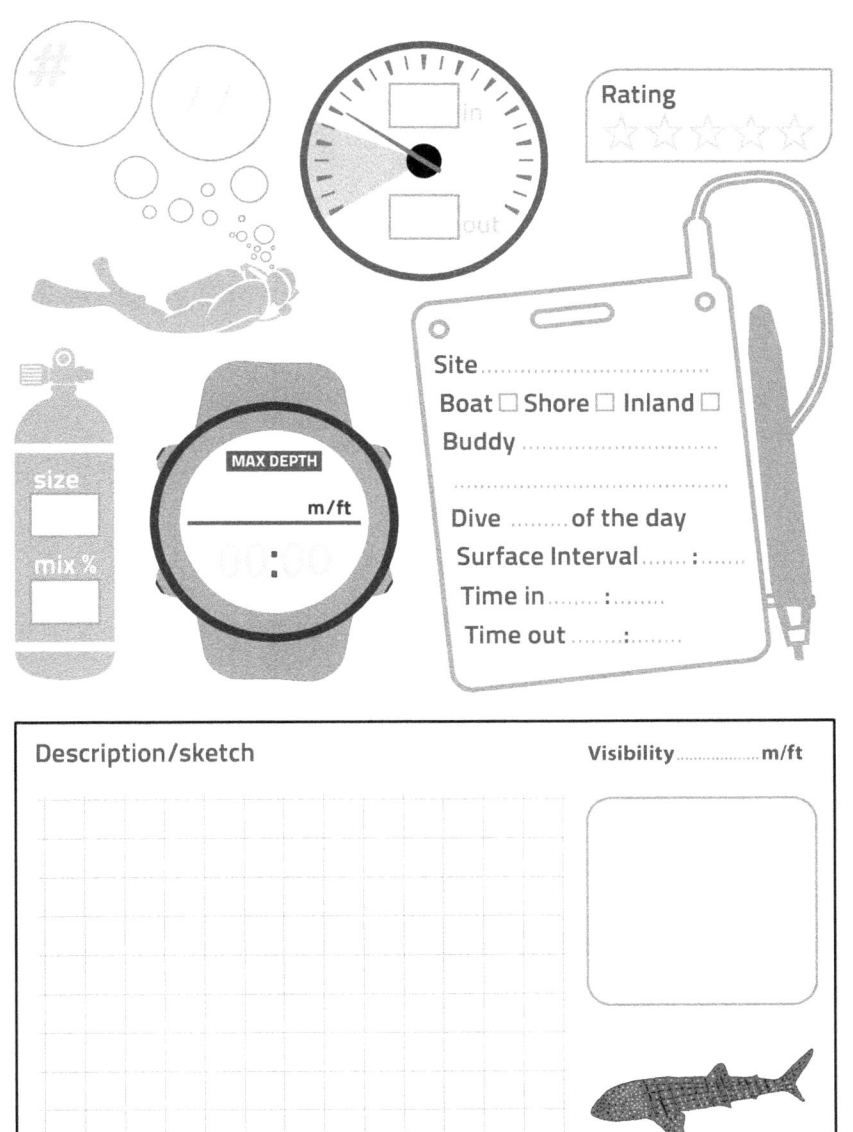

size

mix %

MAX DEPTH
m/ft

Rating

Site..........................
Boat ☐ Shore ☐ Inland ☐
Buddy ....
....
Dive .... of the day
Surface Interval ....:........
Time in ....:........
Time out ....:........

Description/sketch

Visibility .... m/ft

Accumulated Dive Time

Milestone

Verified by

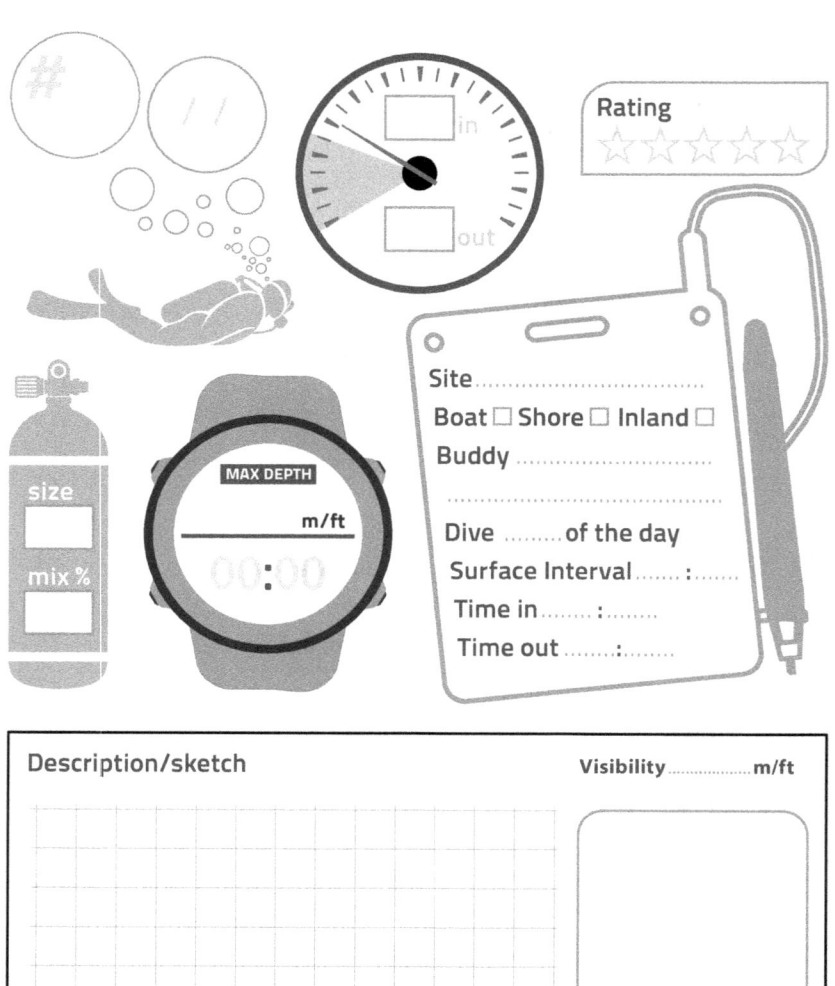

Site ....
Boat ☐ Shore ☐ Inland ☐
Buddy ....

Dive .... of the day
Surface Interval .... : ....
Time in .... : ....
Time out ....:........

size

mix %

MAX DEPTH
m/ft
00:00

Rating ☆☆☆☆☆

Description/sketch   Visibility .... m/ft

Accumulated Dive Time   Milestone   Verified by

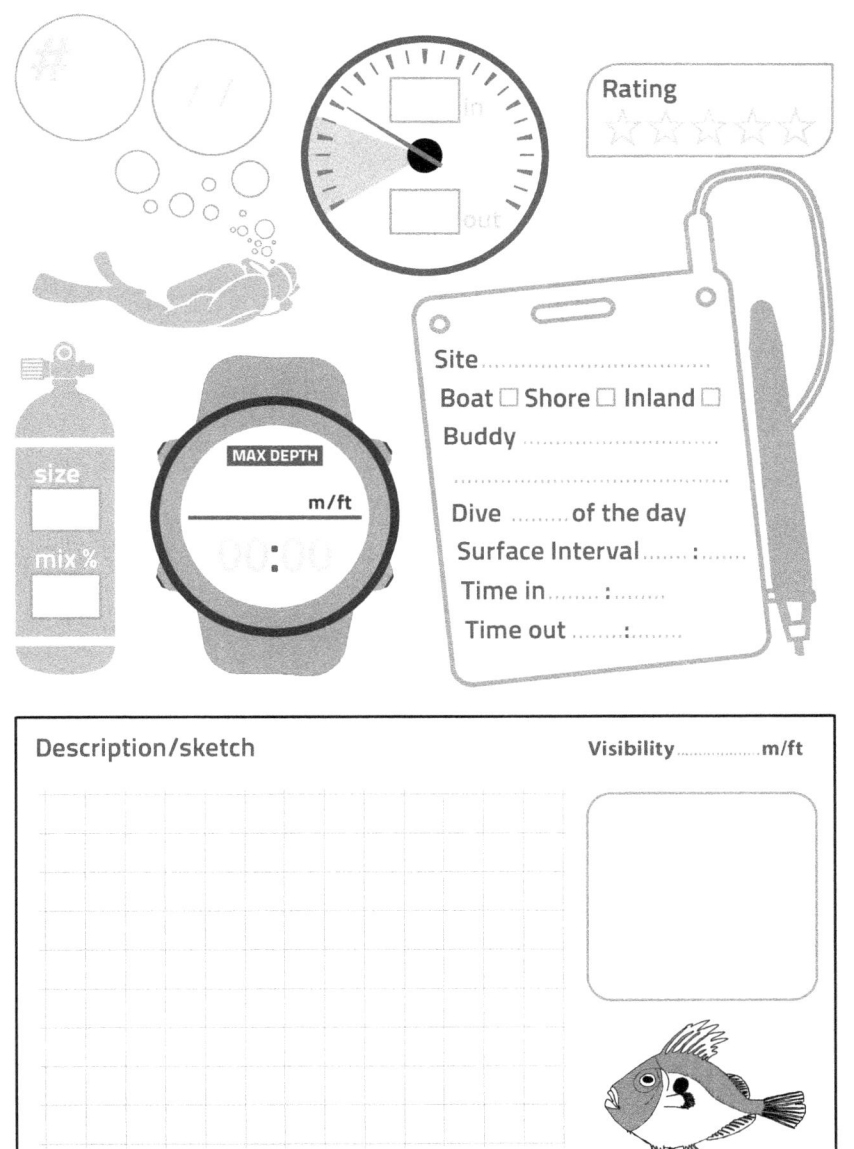

Rating

Site..................................
Boat ☐ Shore ☐ Inland ☐
Buddy ....
....
Dive .... of the day
Surface Interval .... : ....
Time in .... : ....
Time out .... : ....

size

mix %

MAX DEPTH
_____ m/ft

Description/sketch

Visibility .... m/ft

Accumulated Dive Time

.... : ....

Milestone

Verified by

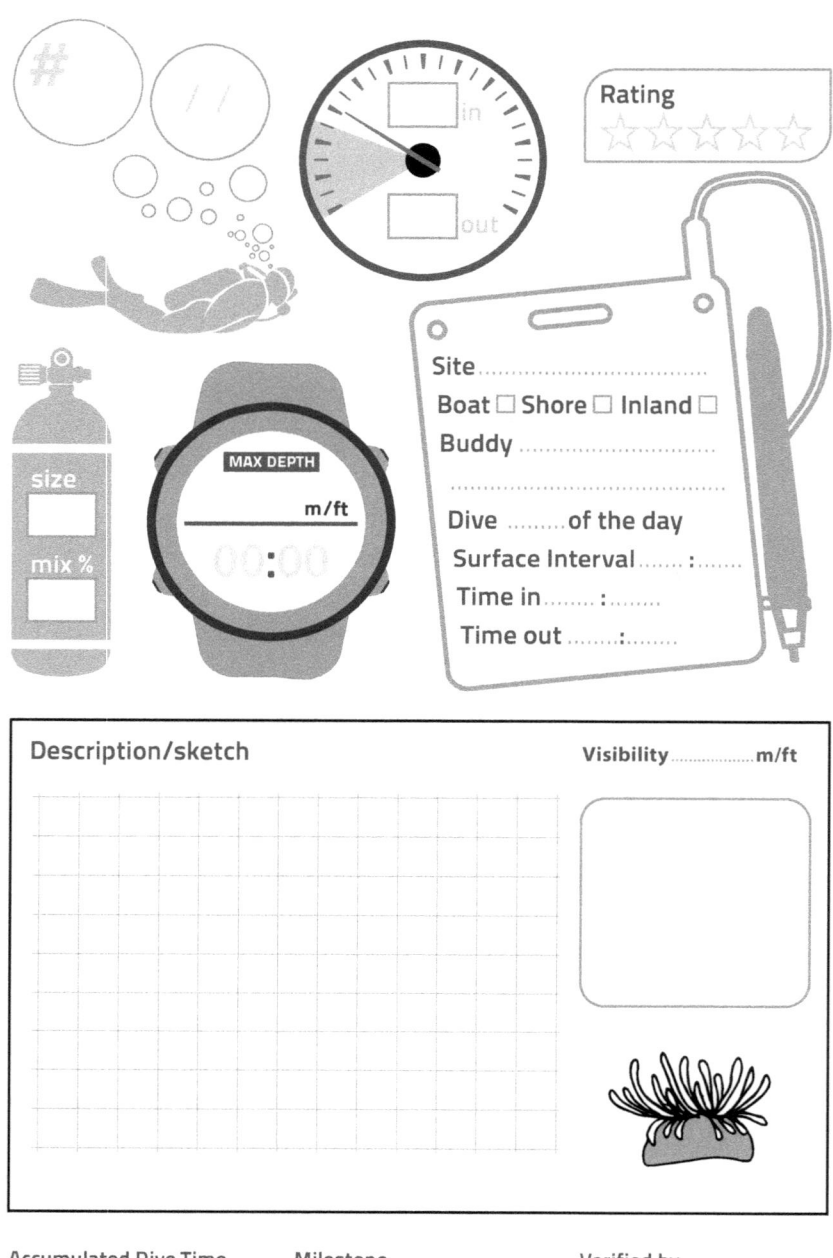

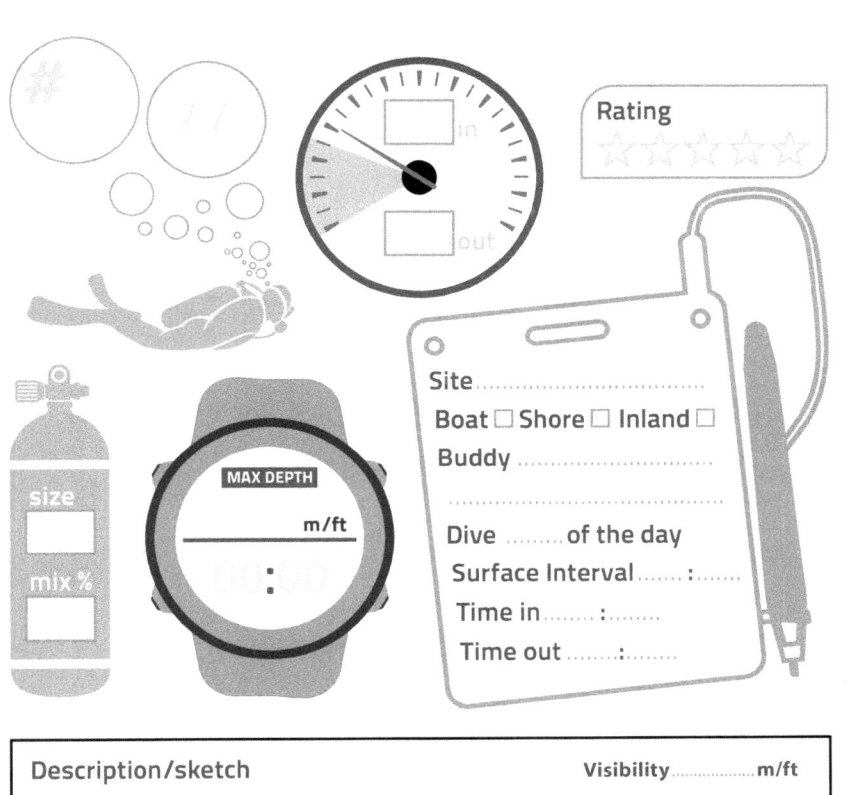

Rating

size

mix %

MAX DEPTH
m/ft

Site..................................
Boat ☐ Shore ☐ Inland ☐
Buddy ....

Dive .... of the day
Surface Interval....... : ....
Time in .... : ....
Time out .... : ....

Description/sketch

Visibility .... m/ft

Accumulated Dive Time

Milestone

Verified by

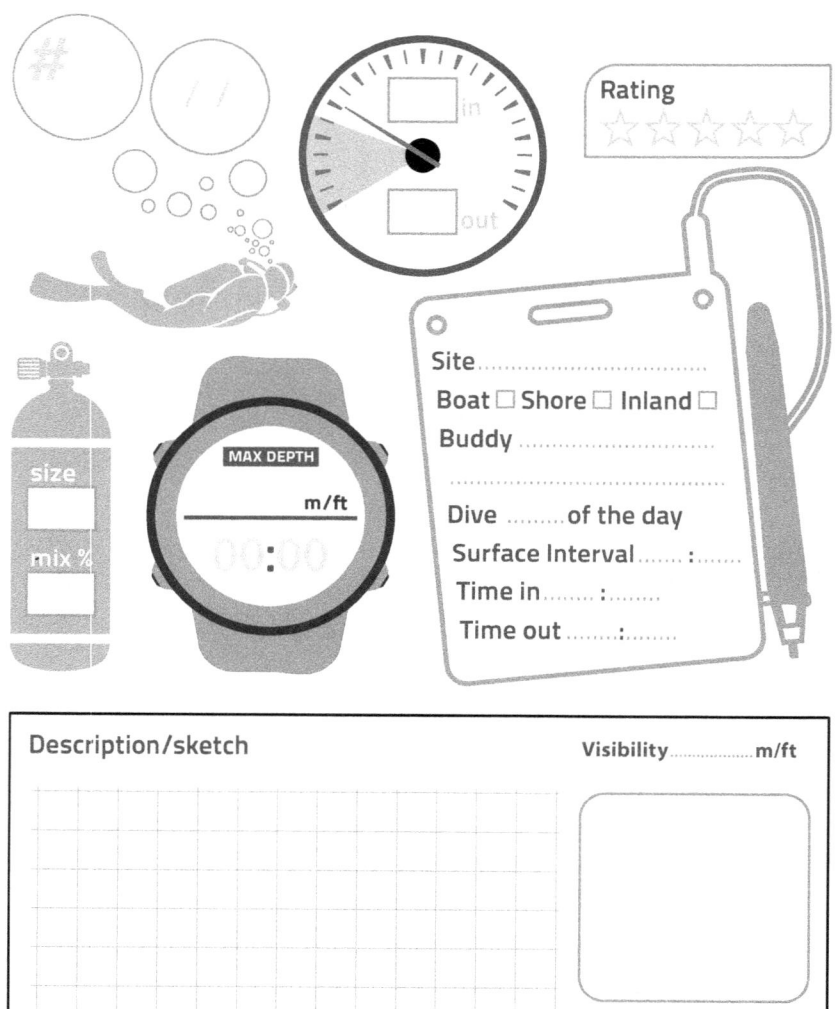

Rating ☆☆☆☆☆

size

mix %

MAX DEPTH
m/ft
00:00

Site.............
Boat ☐ Shore ☐ Inland ☐
Buddy ....
....
Dive .... of the day
Surface Interval .... : ....
Time in .... : ....
Time out .... : ....

Description/sketch

Visibility .... m/ft

Accumulated Dive Time

Milestone

Verified by

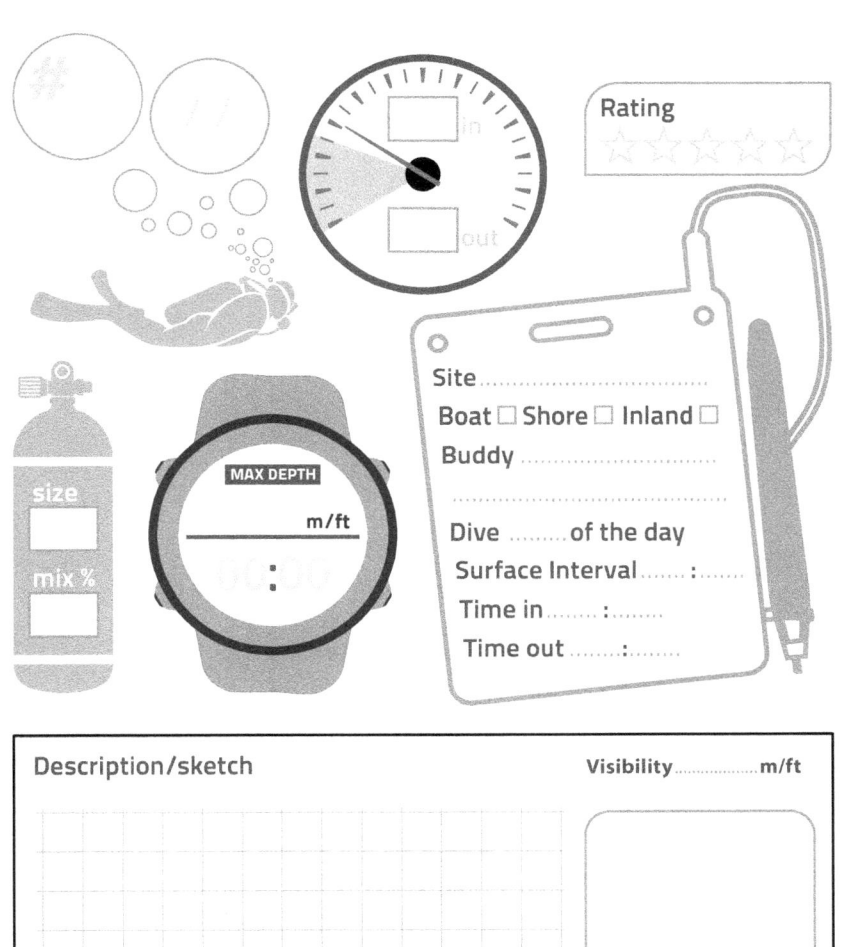

Rating

Site....................................
Boat ☐ Shore ☐ Inland ☐
Buddy ....
....
Dive .... of the day
Surface Interval ...... : ......
Time in .... : ....
Time out .... : ....

MAX DEPTH
m/ft

size
mix %

Description/sketch

Visibility .... m/ft

Accumulated Dive Time   Milestone   Verified by

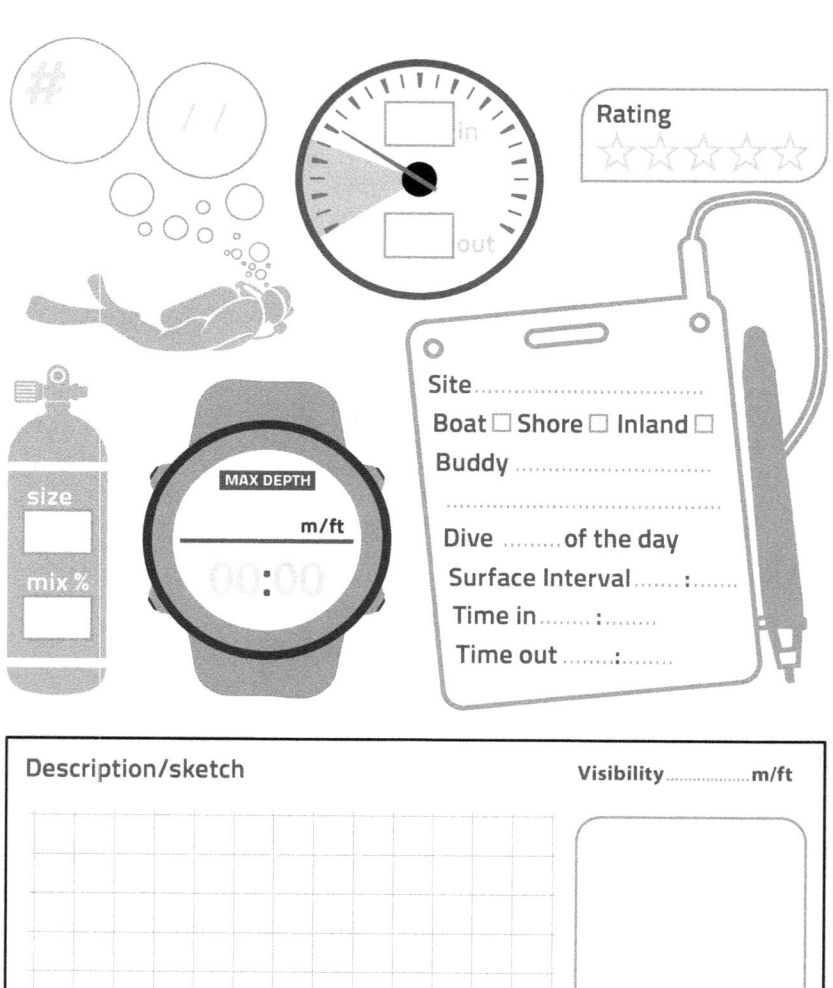

Description/sketch

Visibility .... m/ft

Accumulated Dive Time

....................:....................

Milestone

....

Verified by

....

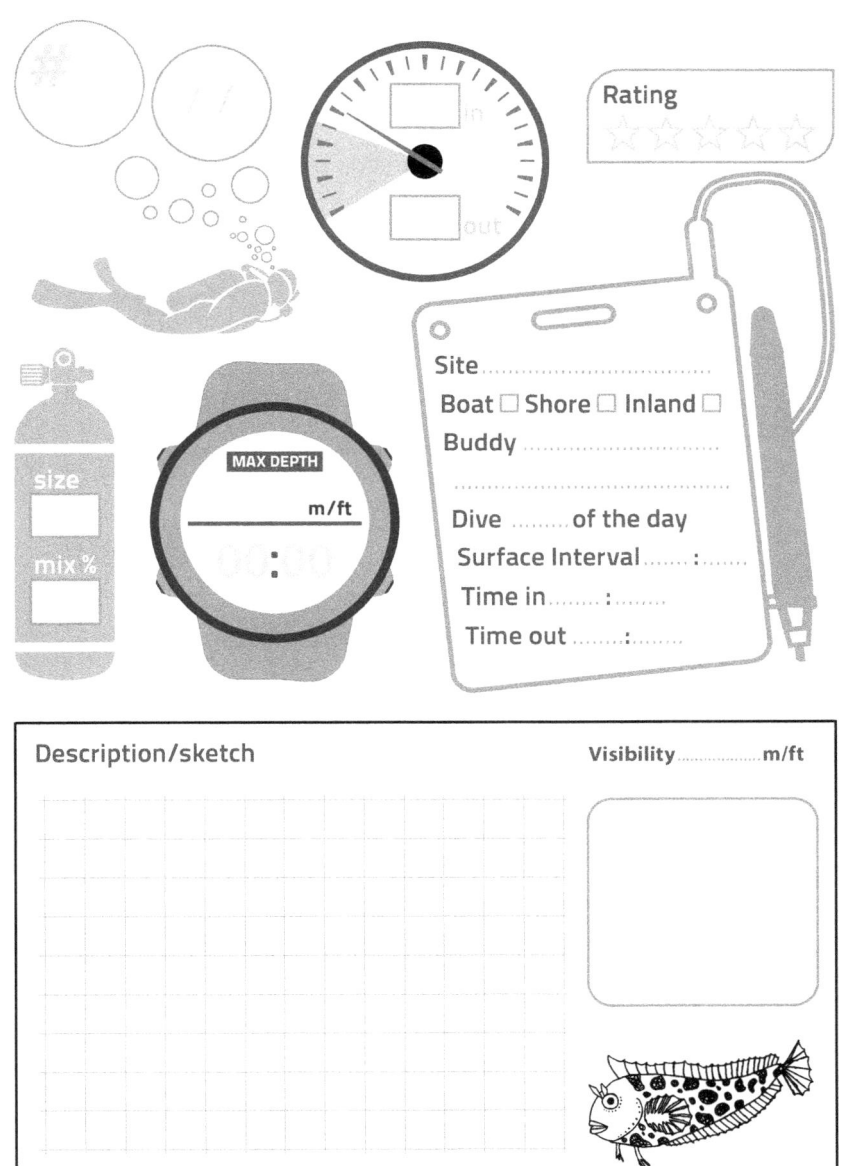

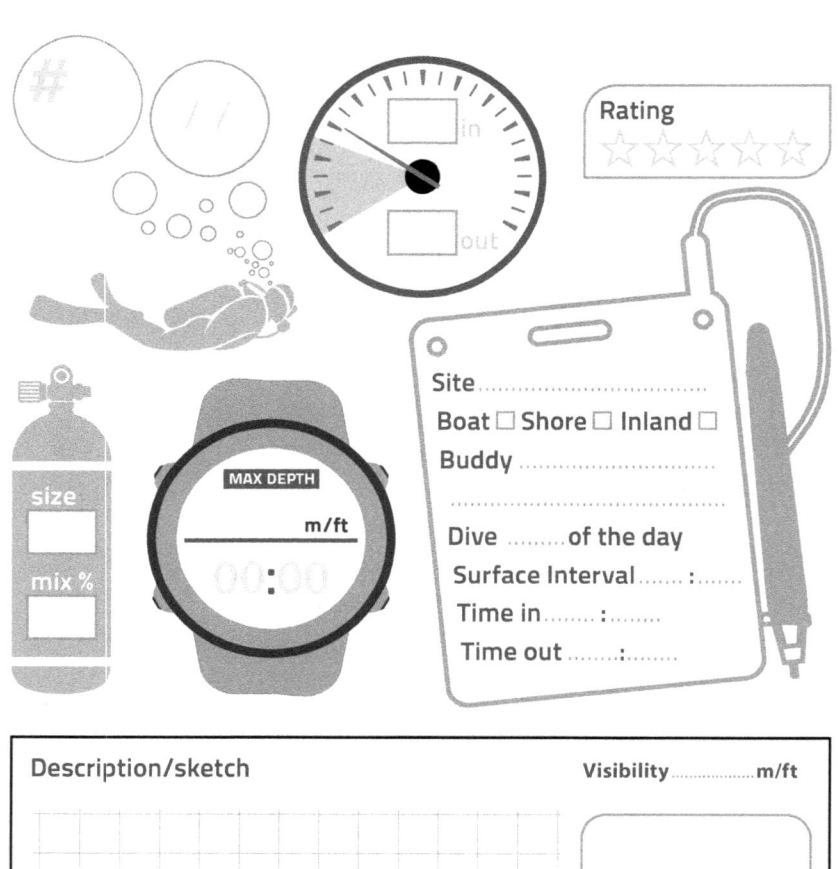

| Description/sketch | Visibility .... m/ft |

Accumulated Dive Time   Milestone   Verified by

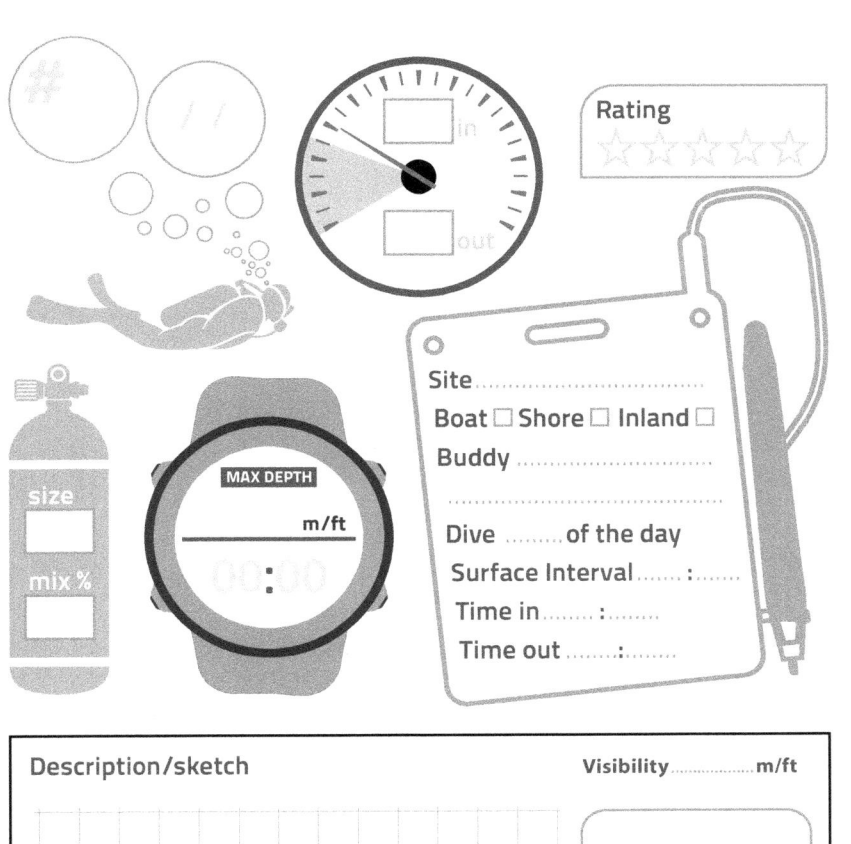

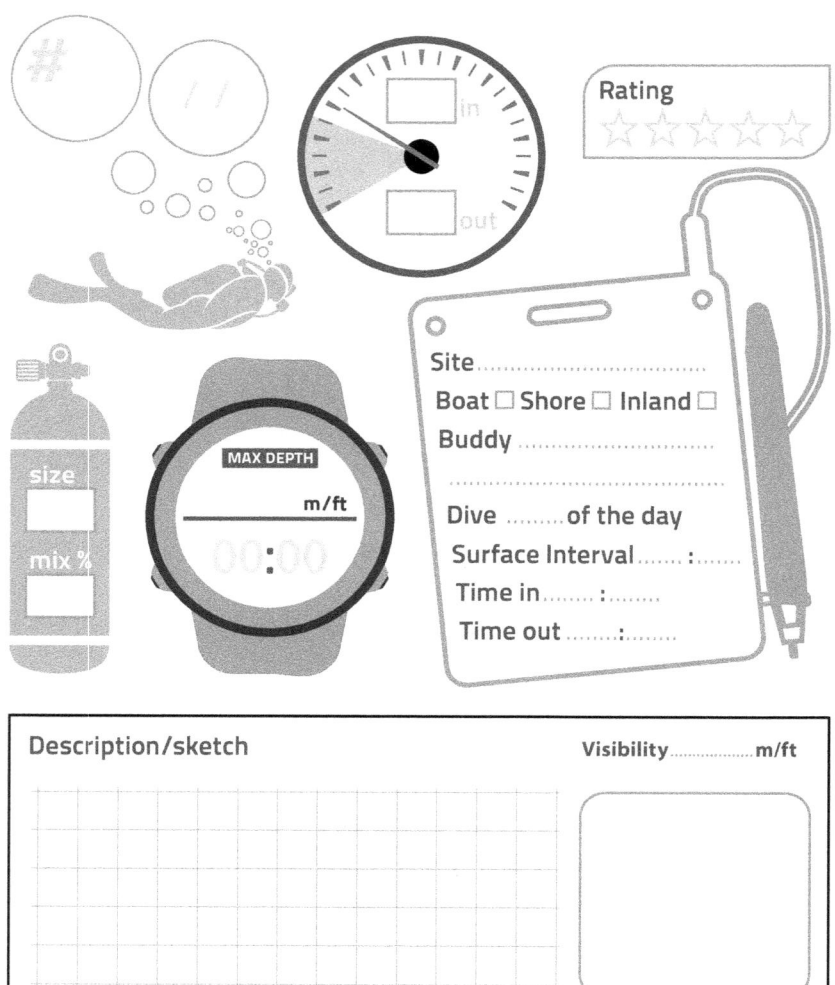

Site..........................
Boat ☐ Shore ☐ Inland ☐
Buddy ....

Dive .... of the day
Surface Interval .... : ....
Time in .... : ....
Time out .... : ....

Rating

MAX DEPTH
m/ft
00:00

size
mix %

Description/sketch   Visibility .... m/ft

Accumulated Dive Time   Milestone   Verified by
.... : ....

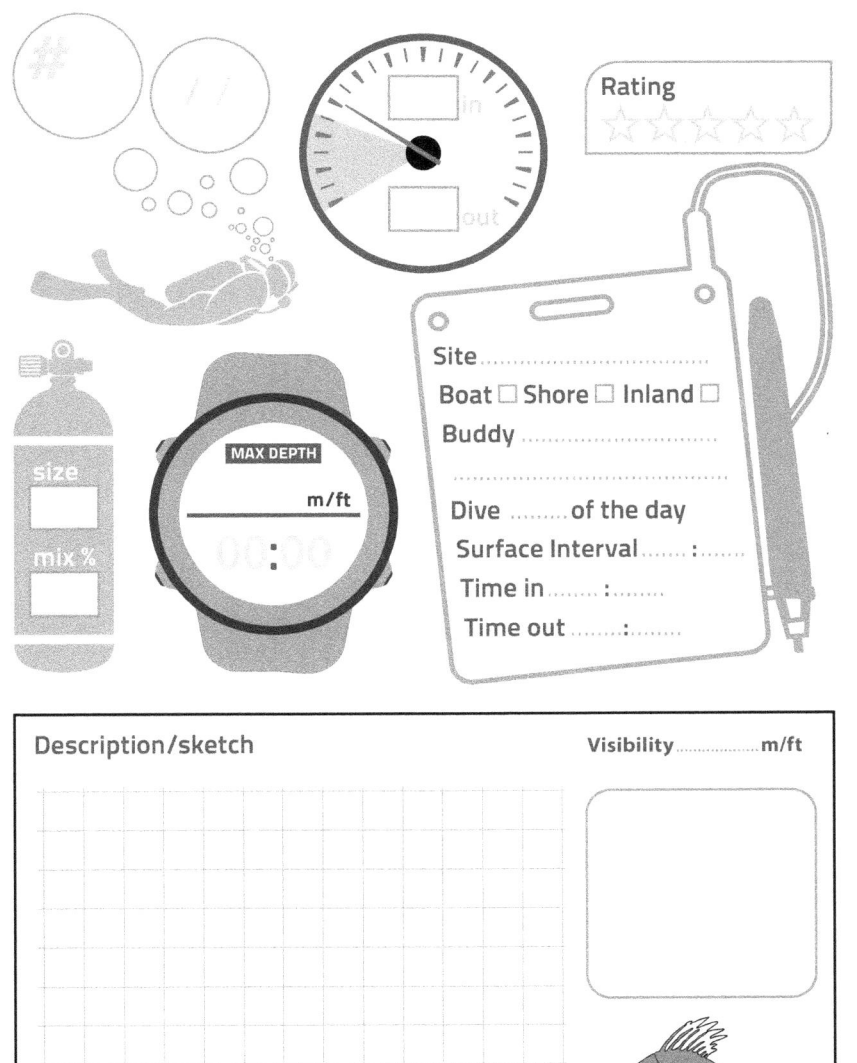

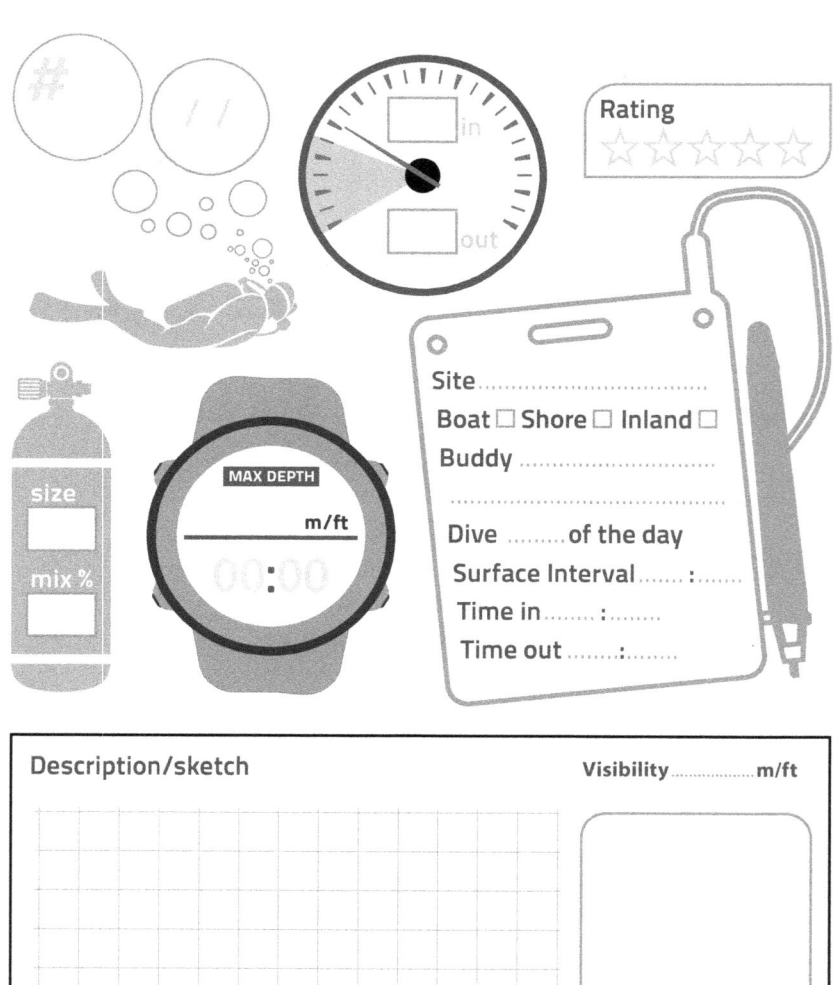

Rating ☆☆☆☆☆

Site....................
Boat ☐ Shore ☐ Inland ☐
Buddy....................
....
Dive .... of the day
Surface Interval .... : ....
Time in .... : ....
Time out .... : ....

MAX DEPTH
m/ft
00:00

size
mix %

Description/sketch Visibility .... m/ft

Accumulated Dive Time Milestone Verified by

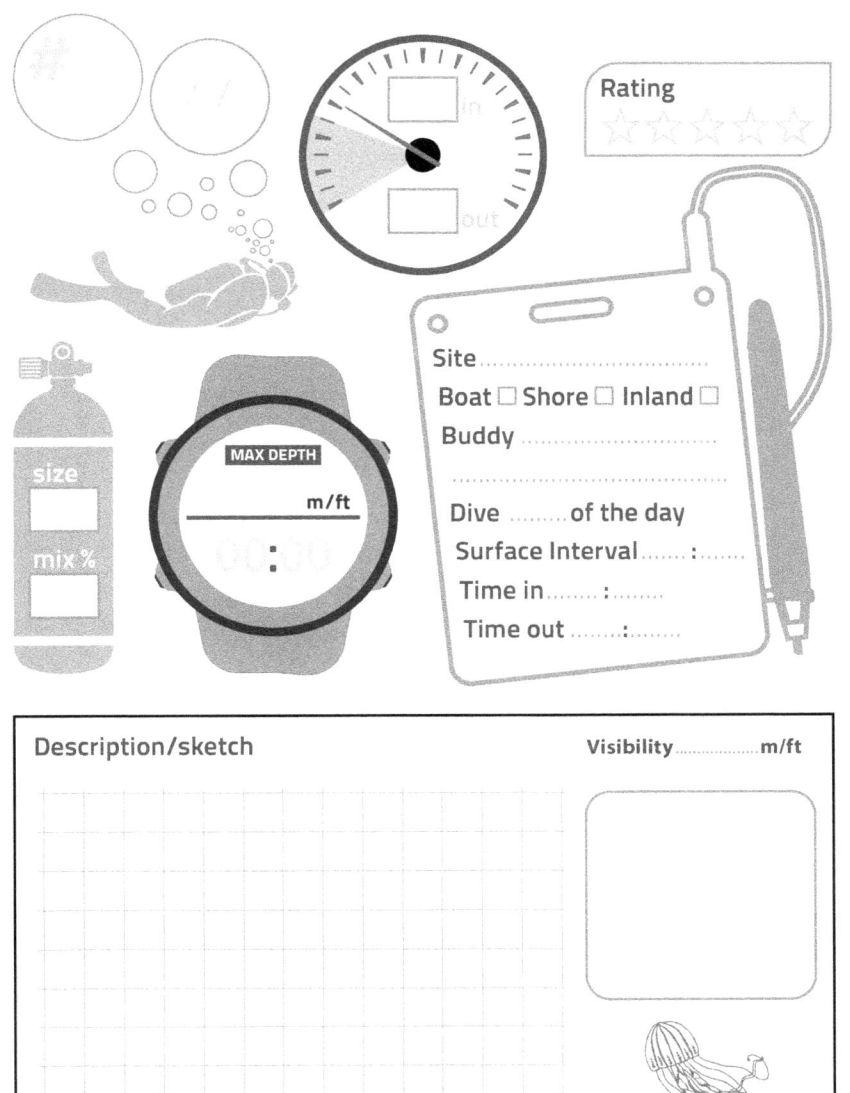

Rating

Site..........
Boat ☐ Shore ☐ Inland ☐
Buddy ....

Dive .... of the day
Surface Interval .... : ....
Time in .... : ....
Time out .... : ....

MAX DEPTH
m/ft

size
mix %

Description/sketch

Visibility .... m/ft

Accumulated Dive Time

Milestone

Verified by

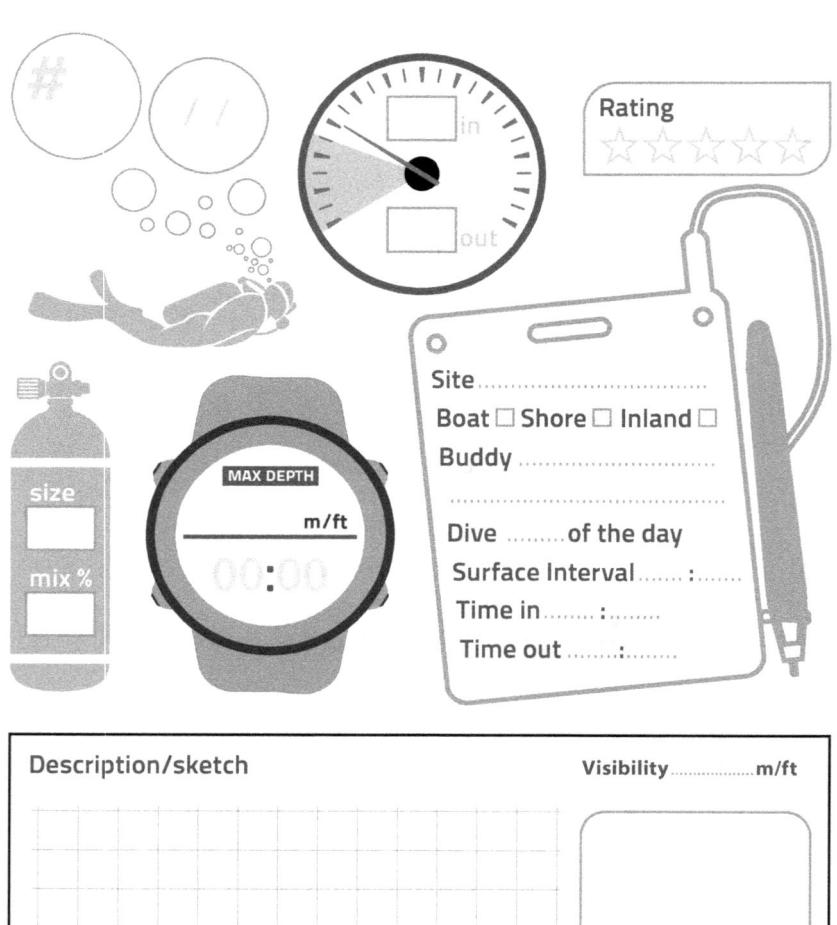

Rating ☆☆☆☆☆		

size

mix %

MAX DEPTH — m/ft
00:00

Site ....
Boat ☐ Shore ☐ Inland ☐
Buddy ....
....
Dive .... of the day
Surface Interval ......:......
Time in ......:......
Time out ......:......

Description/sketch   Visibility .... m/ft

Accumulated Dive Time   Milestone   Verified by
..............:..............

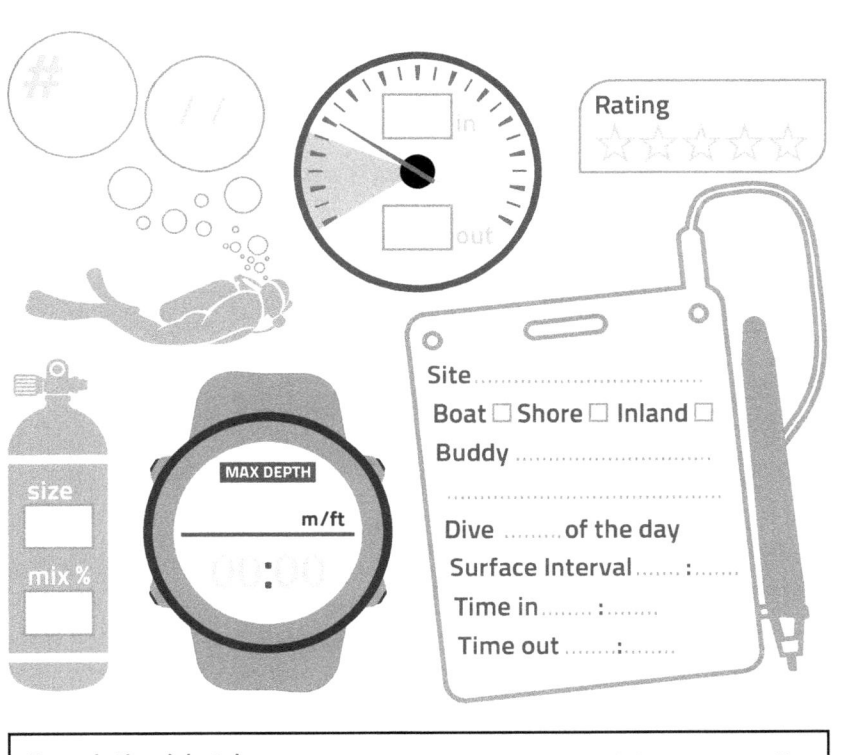

Rating

size

mix %

MAX DEPTH
m/ft

Site..........
Boat ☐ Shore ☐ Inland ☐
Buddy ....

Dive .... of the day
Surface Interval ......:......
Time in ......:......
Time out ......:......

Description/sketch   Visibility................m/ft

Accumulated Dive Time   Milestone   Verified by

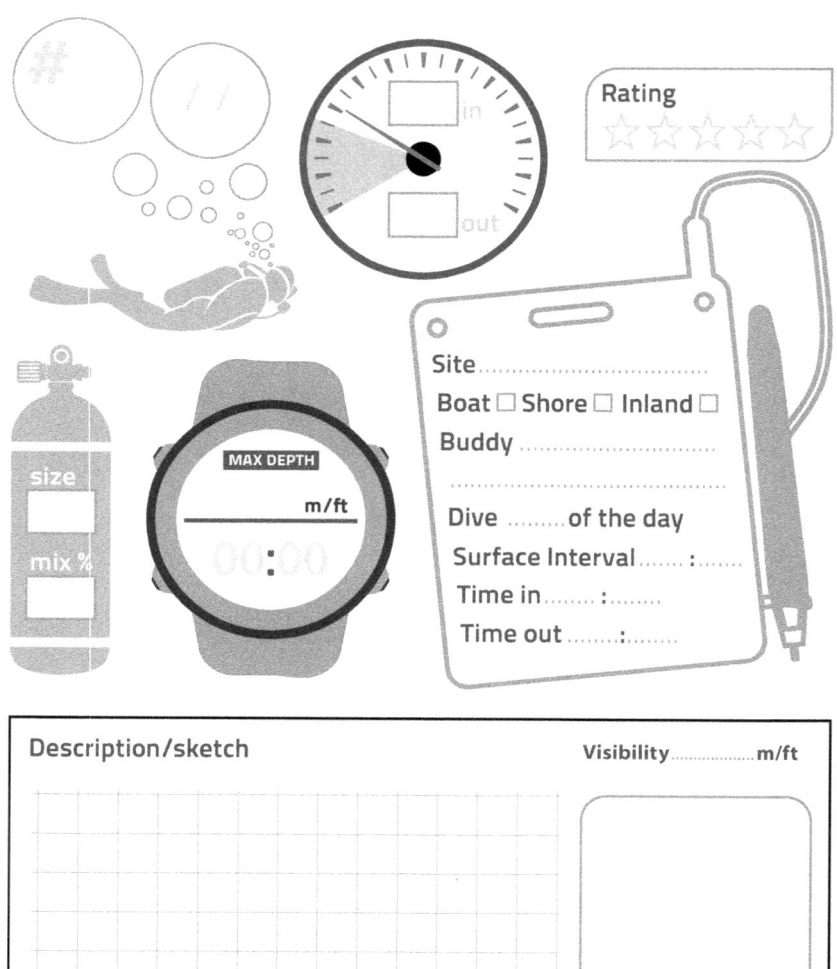

	in
	out

Rating ☆☆☆☆☆

size

mix %

MAX DEPTH

m/ft

00:00

Site..........
Boat ☐ Shore ☐ Inland ☐
Buddy ....
....
Dive .... of the day
Surface Interval........:........
Time in........:........
Time out........:........

Description/sketch

Visibility................m/ft

Accumulated Dive Time

Milestone

Verified by

..........:..........

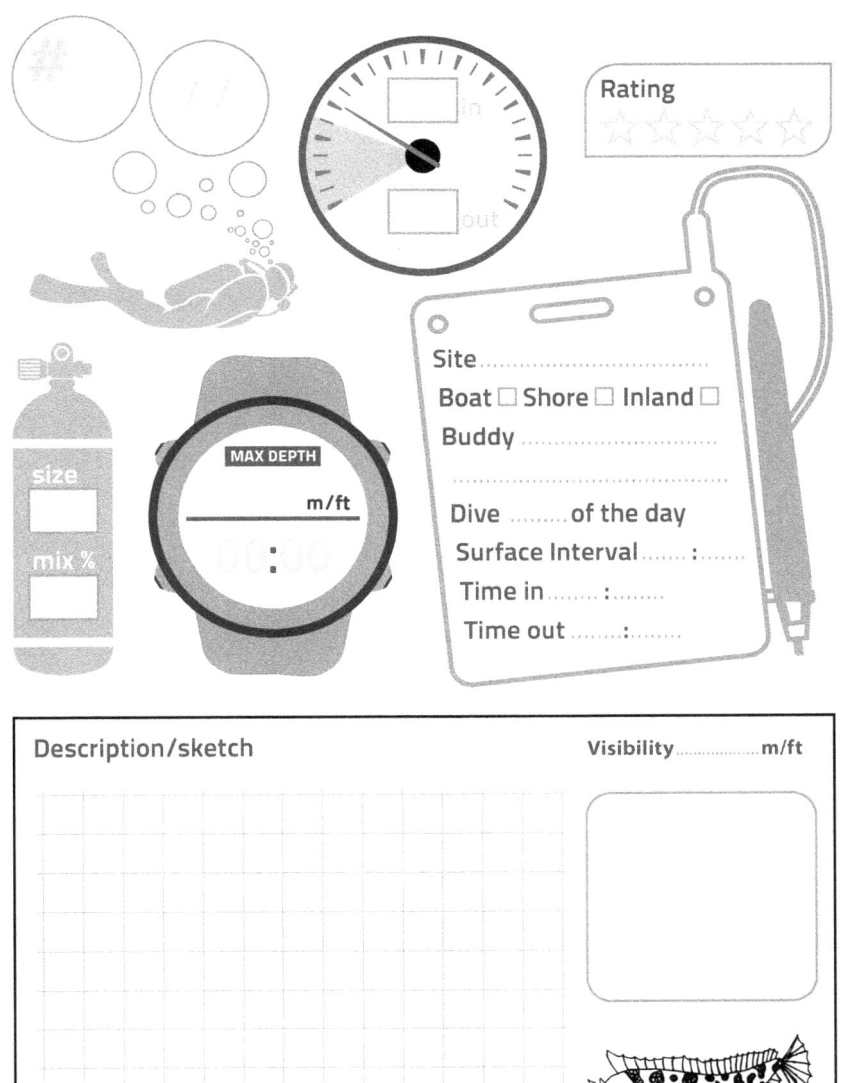

size

mix %

MAX DEPTH m/ft

Rating

Site..............................
Boat ☐ Shore ☐ Inland ☐
Buddy ....
....
Dive .... of the day
Surface Interval .... : ....
Time in .... : ....
Time out .... : ....

Description/sketch

Visibility .... m/ft

Accumulated Dive Time

.... : ....

Milestone

Verified by

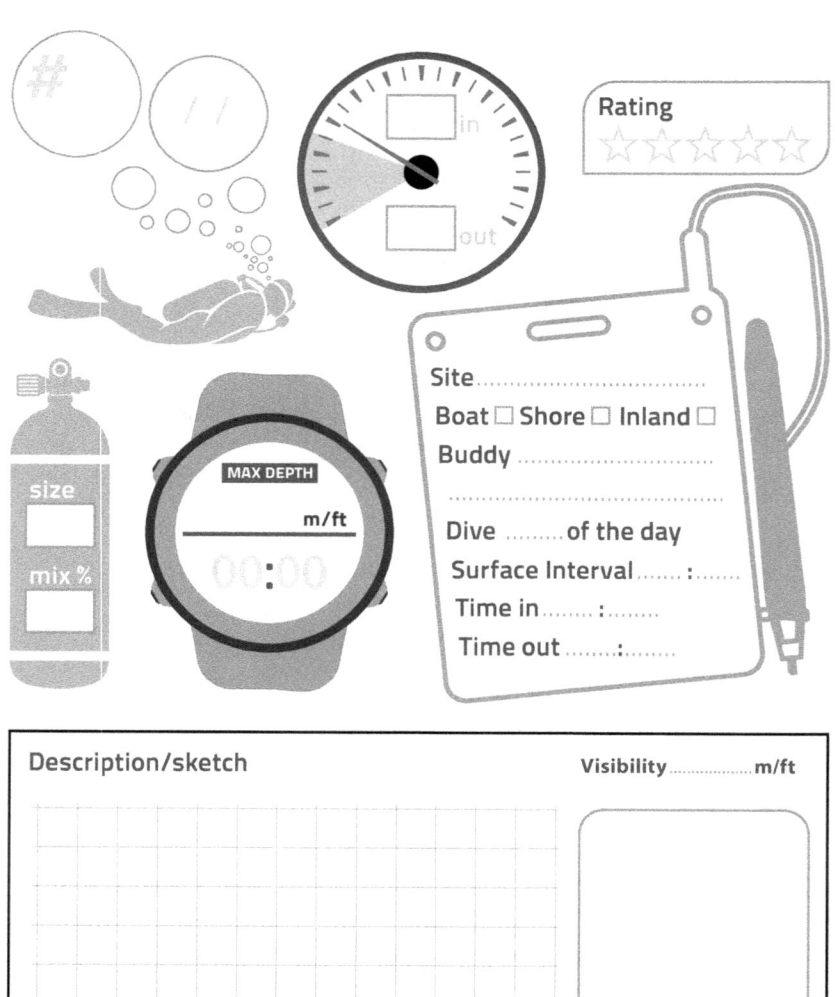

size

mix %

MAX DEPTH

m/ft

00:00

Rating
☆☆☆☆☆

Site ....
Boat ☐ Shore ☐ Inland ☐
Buddy ....

Dive .... of the day
Surface Interval .... : ....
Time in .... : ....
Time out .... : ....

Description/sketch	Visibility .... m/ft

Accumulated Dive Time   Milestone   Verified by

.... : ....

NOTES

Diving Gozo & Comino

The essential guide to an underwater playground
by Richard Salter

'A very good guide'— *Diver*

Paperback & Ebook | ISBN 978-1-909455-16-0

Diving Equipment

Choice, maintenance and function
by Jonas Arvidsson

'Should be on every diver's bookshelf'—*Diver*

Paperback & Ebook | ISBN 978-1-909455-13-9

Winning Images with *ANY* Underwater Camera

The Essential Guide to Creating Engaging Photos
by Paul Colley, with a Foreword by Alex Mustard

'For all underwater photographers who want to get ahead of the game'— *UWP Magazine*

'Will arm and inspire you to transform your underwater photographs, whatever camera you use'— *Alex Mustard*

Paperback and Ebook | ISBN 978-1-909455-04-7

For more details and to order go to **DivedUp.com**

BOOKS FOR UNDERWATER EXPLORERS

The Diver's Tale
by Nick Lyon

'That rare thing in diving – a very funny book'— *Diver*

'...such an enjoyable read'— *Scuba Diver*

'A brilliantly British book, full of heart and humour'— *BritishDiver.co.uk*

Paperback & Ebook | ISBN 978-1-909455-24-5

The Forgotten Shipwreck
Solving the Mystery of the Darlwyne
by Nick Lyon

'As with all Nick's books, this is well written and extremely well researched. Nick tells a good story with realism and when appropriate, a touch of humour... Nick takes us on a fascinating journey to find the lost wreck and try, finally, to give the surviving family and friends some closure'— *Scubaverse*

Paperback & Ebook | ISBN 978-1-909455-31-3

 For more details and to order go to **DivedUp.com**

www.ingramcontent.com/pod-product-compliance
Lightning Source LLC
Chambersburg PA
CBHW061514040426
42450CB00008B/1619